PICTORIAL QUILTS

Noted fabric artist Margaret Cusack used brocades, gingham, satin, and knit fabrics for her appliquéd collage *Still Life*, 11" x 14" (28cm x 36cm), which was done for an illustration in *Cue* magazine, and then as a *Reader's Digest* cover.
Photographer: Ron Breland; Owner: Jack Miller.

D0624672

OTHER BOOKS AVAILABLE FROM CHILTON

Robbie Fanning, Series Editor

Contemporary Quilting Series

Appliqué the Ann Boyce Way, by Ann Boyce
Contemporary Quilting Techniques, by Pat Cairns
Fast Patch, by Anita Hallock
Fourteen Easy Baby Quilts, by Margaret Dittman
Machine-Quilted Jackets, Vests, and Coats, by Nancy Moore
Precision-Pieced Quilts Using the Foundation Method, by Jane Hall and Dixie Haywood
The Quilter's Guide to Rotary Cutting, by Donna Poster
Quilts by the Slice, by Beckie Olson
Scrap Quilts Using Fast Patch, by Anita Hallock
Speed-Cut Quilts, by Donna Poster
Super Simple Quilts, by Kathleen Eaton
Teach Yourself Machine Piecing and Quilting, by Debra Wagner
Three-Dimensional Appliqué, by Jodie Davis

Creative Machine Arts Series

ABCs of Serging, by Tammy Young and Lori Bottom
The Button Lover's Book, by Marilyn Green
Claire Shaeffer's Fabric Sewing Guide
The Complete Book of Machine Embroidery, by Robbie and Tony Fanning
Creative Nurseries Illustrated, by Debra Terry and Juli Plooster
Creative Serging Illustrated, by Pati Palmer, Gail Brown, and Sue Green
Distinctive Serger Gifts and Crafts, by Naomi Baker and Tammy Young
The Fabric Lover's Scrapbook, by Margaret Dittman
Friendship Quilts by Hand and Machine, by Carolyn Vosburg Hall
Gifts Galore, by Jane Warnick and Jackie Dodson
How to Make Soft Jewelry, by Jackie Dodson
Innovative Serging, by Gail Brown and Tammy Young
Innovative Sewing, by Gail Brown and Tammy Young
Owner's Guide to Sewing Machines, Sergers, and Knitting Machines, by Gale Grigg Hazen
Petite Pizzazz, by Barb Griffin
Putting on the Glitz, by Sandra L. Hatch and Ann Boyce
Serged Garments in Minutes, by Tammy Young and Naomi Baker

Sew Sensational Gifts, by Naomi Baker and Tammy Young
Sew, Serge, Press, by Jan Saunders
Sewing and Collecting Vintage Fashions, by Eileen MacIntosh
Simply Serge Any Fabric, by Naomi Baker and Tammy Young
Soft Gardens, by Yvonne Perez-Collins
Twenty Easy Machine-Made Rugs, by Jackie Dodson

Know Your Sewing Machine Series, by Jackie Dodson

Know Your Bernina, second edition
Know Your Brother, with Jane Warnick
Know Your Elna, with Carol Ahles
Know Your New Home, with Judi Cull and Vicki Lynn Hastings
Know Your Pfaff, with Audrey Griese
Know Your Sewing Machine
Know Your Singer
Know Your Viking, with Jan Saunders
Know Your White, with Jan Saunders

Know Your Serger Series, by Tammy Young and Naomi Baker

Know Your baby lock
Know Your Pfaff Hobbylock
Know Your Serger
Know Your White Superlock

Teach Yourself to Sew Better Series, by Jan Saunders

A Step-by-Step Guide to Your Bernina
A Step-by-Step Guide to Your New Home
A Step-by-Step Guide to Your Sewing Machine
A Step-by-Step Guide to Your Viking

Open Chain Books

Gail Brown's All-New Instant Interiors, by Gail Brown
Jane Asher's Costume Book, by Gail Brown
Learn Bearmaking, by Judi Maddigan
Quick Napkin Creations, by Gail Brown
Sew Any Patch Pocket, by Claire Shaeffer
Singer Instructions for Art Embroidery and Lace Work
Soft Toys for Babies, by Judi Maddigan

Crafts Kaleidoscope

Fabric Painting Made Easy, by Nancy Ward
How to Make Cloth Books for Children, by Anne Pellowski
Quick and Easy Ways With Ribbon, by Ceci Johnson

VIC APR 29 1994

PICTORIAL QUILTS

Carolyn Vosburg Hall

Chilton Book Company

Radnor, Pennsylvania

Victorville Branch Library
15011 Circle Drive
Victorville, CA 92392

SAN BERNARDINO
COUNTY LIBRARY
SAN BERNARDINO, CA

ACKNOWLEDGMENTS

W riting this book was something like assembling a quilting bee of skillful and energetic helpers to contribute blocks and to help stitch the layers together into a finished product, and I want to thank them all. First are the members of the Art Quilt Network-New York and other fiber artists who so generously contributed their innovative works for inclusion in this book. My granddaughter, six-year-old Hattie Stroud, got busy and made a quilt full of designs for chapter 8. Lori Hirsch Tennent dragged in trunks of lighting equipment to do color and black-and-white photography. Robbie Fanning—who has more energy than six ordinary people—serves as editor for this series. At Chilton, Susan Clarey acquired the book and editor Kathy Conover helped wrestle through details on photo reproduction, diagram size, text length, and more. Many unsung people worked to produce the finished book, and thanks go to them too. If the book is engineer-clear, you can thank my husband, Cap Hall, for his input.

This book is dedicated to my mother, Doris Vosburg, with whom I spent many happy hours roaming the aisles at Cloth World.

Copyright © 1993 by Carolyn Vosburg Hall

All Rights Reserved

Published in Radnor, Pennsylvania 19089, by Chilton Book Company

No part of this book may be reproduced, transmitted or stored in any form or by any means, electronic or mechanical, without prior written permission from the publisher

Designed by Rosalyn Carson

Photographs by Carolyn Vosburg Hall and Laurie Hirsch Tennent except where otherwise noted.

Line drawings by Carolyn Vosburg Hall

Production by Rosalie Cooke

Manufactured in the United States of America

ISBN: 0-8019-8245-6

Library of Congress Catalog Card No: 92-56583

1 2 3 4 5 6 7 8 9 0   2 1 0 9 8 7 6 5 4 3

CONTENTS

❖

FOREWORD

W ith luck, nurturing, and persistence, we all have a chance to develop our special talents. The child who always drew comic book characters becomes an illustrator. The one who organized backyard play goes into the theater. And the one like me, who wrote skits for school rallies, becomes a writer.

For me, writing is as natural as breathing. When I get an idea, usually in the form of a question, I'm off and running: Why does polyester thread kink and knot when I'm hand-hemming? I start thinking about it while I'm driving, doing the dishes, or walking. Then I begin to assemble support for answers: experimentation, books, articles, friends, and experts. I make notes, research, draft, rewrite, and eventually write a comprehensive article on thread.

Designing, however, is extremely difficult for me. I get a vague idea, make a rough unsatisfactory sketch, and give up, thinking, "I wish I could design better."

Carolyn Vosburg Hall's book, *Pictorial Quilts*, has opened my mind. Suddenly I realize I'm not working smart enough. I need to think about possibilities more, assemble support, use the tools available to me. That's what all designers do, I now realize.

It's not as if they have a world of images stored in their heads like a massive CD-ROM: stare at a piece of paper, extract needed images, draw on paper, and...voilà! the finished design.

No, it's a step-by-step process of making choices from the assembled material, all of which Carolyn carefully details in this inspiring book.

Aren't we lucky that Carolyn Hall's special talents include quilting, designing, and writing?

Robbie Fanning
Series Editor

Are you interested in a quarterly newsletter about creative uses of the sewing machine and serger, edited by Robbie Fanning? Write to The Creative Machine, PO Box 2634-B, Menlo Park, CA 94026.

QUILTS MOVE OFF THE BED

Introduction

"I saw a wonderful quilt show," a designer friend said, "but none of those quilts would fit on a bed." More and more artists are using quilting as a technique to make stitchery artworks rather than bed quilts. All of the pieces in this book show pictorial imagery and all are quilted; that is sewn of fabrics in layered construction. Most are meant to be displayed on a wall rather than on a bed since rumpling distorts the imagery. Others, though, are meant to be used as real quilts, pillows, clothing, or tote bags. What groups them all together is the tactile pleasure that quilted fabrics lend and the visual appeal that imagery gives.

Who is this book for? It's for stitchers who want to know about art: how to represent objects, how to select colors, how to arrange picture space. It's for artists who want to know about stitching: how to sew by hand and/or machine, how to select fabrics and threads, and how to appliqué, embroider, and more. It is for those who get pleasure and ideas from photos showing what's going on in this field. And it is for people who want to do projects with the patterns and directions provided. Of course this book cannot contain all there is to know about everything, so the Sources section offers additional resource information.

Making pictorial quilting doesn't call for complicated equipment or remarkable talent, although both are handy to have. You can simply take up your needle, thread, fabrics, and scissors and begin. If hand sewing is too slow, plug in your sewing machine, clip out a pile of appliqué pieces, and push the pedal: or use fabric crayons for quick results; or transfer photographs to fabric blocks and quilt them together. A variety of techniques is given for you to try. You needn't make a king-size quilt at first. Choose a smaller size and show your masterpiece as a wall hanging. If all you have is fifteen minutes at a time and you still want a big quilt or you want to do slower techniques such as English piecing, make your quilt in short stints day after day. That's also how children are raised, novels are written, and skyscrapers are built.

The artists' works shown here provide a gold mine of techniques and ideas to inspire you. No matter how impossibly complex an artist's technique might seem, it may contain something usable for you. An idea can serve as a starting point for your imagination. The description of a technique might set you afire. Yet making the initial design decisions takes time and effort. You can begin instead with re-creating one of the projects. This way you learn the process, create something you can enjoy, and develop confidence by your accomplishment.

Most of the examples included were created by artists who belong to the Art Quilt Network—New York, a national group of artists who make art using fabric and stitching. Member Margaret Cusack, whose work has appeared in my books over the years, contributed much help and many wonderful examples. I love the way her brain works. She, like many stitchery artists, is bright, humorous, talented, and generous, and these qualities show in her creations. In addition, I've quoted several artists when possible to show how they think and work.

In these pages, you will see an inspiring variety of ways to apply designs to fabrics, from a six-year-old's quilt to nationally respected fiber artists' artworks. You will discover that you can find visual imagery anywhere. Margaret Cusack finds it in the kitchen for her fabric collage that was used as a magazine illustration (half-title page). Nancy Jane Collins pictures her farm (on this page), and Tafi Brown glorifies nature in *Tree IV: All Seasons* (on following page).

Nancy Jane Collins lives on a farm tending thousands of chickens while creating these delightful Grandma Moses-style quilt pictures, including this unnamed commission for the Minnesota Farm Credit Services. Grandma Moses was the noted American primitive painter Anna Mary Moses, née Robertson. Photographer: Burge Photography.

It is what you do with the imagery that counts. You can simplify, elaborate, combine, translate, or rework it in a variety of ways. Ideas, images, and techniques can be used simply or as intricately as you wish to accomplish your effects.

HOW TO USE THIS BOOK

Creativity is not a neat process. It is artists using fibers to make art, quilters using artistic imagery to make stitcheries, and others using any technique at hand to carry out their ideas. Ideally, you need to learn everything at once—the artist's visual techniques, the stitcher's sewing techniques, and the general philosophy of the art form.

For this reason, an assortment of art and sewing techniques comes interwoven with concepts and opinions as they seem to fit. The nine chapters follow steps in the artistic process, from developing imagery through designing the parts, arranging space,

and using drafting techniques to constructing stitcheries using elements of art, such as space, line, shape, color, texture and form. Each chapter features a project that allows you the choice of hands-on experience to make as directed, or to use the techniques involved in your own way. The first project in chapter 1, for example, shows a mix of drawing and sewing techniques while other projects use techniques for transferring, drawing, appliquéing, piecing, quilting, and embroidering by hand and machine.

You can look at the pictures, decide what ideas you want to try, and read how artists created their scenes in the related text. Whenever I write a book like this featuring artists' exciting examples and inventive techniques, more ideas come than I could develop in a lifetime. I hope this book inspires you in the same way.

Tafi Brown loves the New Hampshire woods, using them for photographic flip-flopped imagery in her cyanotype blueprinted quilt, Trees IV: All Seasons *74-1/2" x 46" (189cm x 117cm)*

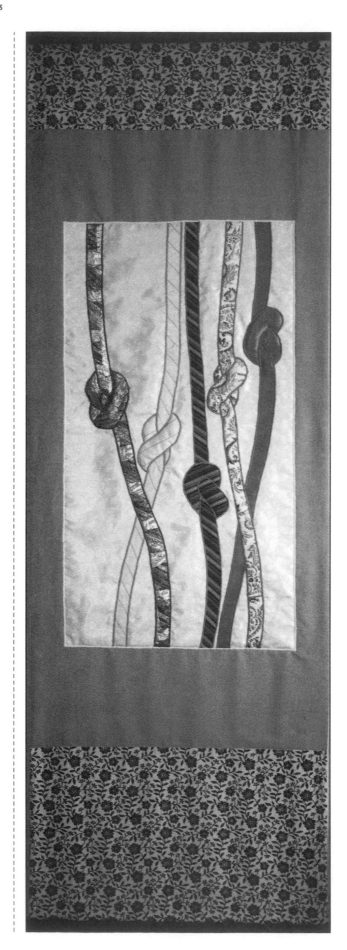

1-1. Knot Kakimono *by the author shows simple imagery on a traditional Japanese scroll shape. Instructions for making this are provided in the project section at the end of chapter 1. Photo: Author.*

IMAGERY: CREATING IDEAS
Chapter One

Making a picture quilt delights the eye, entertains the hand, and challenges the mind. This adds up to heaven for a lot of us. So whether you are a traditional quilt maker, a contemporary fiber artist, or an enthusiastic amateur, you can aim to create a serious work of art, or to knock out a piece just for the pleasure. This book gives you a variety of techniques for creating and constructing designs. Of course, you'll find yourself coming up with new ideas on your own.

This first chapter describes the kinds of imagery you can put on fabrics, suggests how to find ideas for that imagery, and tells about drawing images and making patterns. The project *Knot Kakimono* (Fig. 1-1), shows how a simple idea—in this case, a knot in a string—can be used to create a stitchery and gives instructions for machine appliqué, satin-stitching, and assembling a wall hanging.

GETTING IDEAS
Imagining

Let's start with making real an idea in your mind. In Fig. 1-2, you know that the Mexican embroidered flowers on the dress or the elephant from Thailand are made of floss or sequins, yet you also accept them as images. To make a picture quilt, what your eyes see—whether garden flowers or an elephant's bulk—must be translated into flat designs and materials to be applied to fabrics. The same is true for any art form: the painter must change visions in his or her mind to lines and shapes in paint, the printmaker to inks, and the stitcher to threads.

Imagery can be presented in endless ways. The flowers in Fig. 1-2 show similarities and differences, from the free-flowing Malaysian batik to the geometric Mexican embroideries. There's no one right way to translate ideas into fabric designs. Over the thousands of years that people have made art, different cultural groups have invented different kinds of traditional imagery. The materials they use shape their designs, their beliefs affect their imagery, and the way they construct their creations influences the results.

It's the same with contemporary stitchers. We have almost too many sources for inspiration, considering all the ideas and images from the past and present combined with the materials and supplies of today. We can put almost any imagery we can imagine on fabric. Let's narrow this to the technical and aesthetic process of seeing.

1-2. Pictorial imagery is used on six ethnic textiles: (clockwise from top left) sequined elephant from Thailand, Malaysian batik skirt, Mexican embroidered dress, belt from Pakistan (across the dress), Chinese couched embroidered bird, and Hmong (Laos) reverse appliqué.

Seeing

The camera has affected the way people see. It snaps a scene from one viewpoint and freezes it in place. Our eyes recognize a scene as realistic if it looks like a camera took it. However, there are other ways to see. Human eyes might not be able to locate a mouse in a field from one hundred feet away, as a hawk can, but they can see a picture in a book which is a cluster of tiny black ink dots, and know what it means—which our dogs and cats can't do.

Seeing is a two-part process. Your eyes take in the scene and then your brain decides what to make of it. A child sees a wild daisy as a flower to pick for her mother. A young man sees the same flower as a romantic test: she loves me, she loves me not. A gardener sees the errant daisy as a weed in his grass. Give yourself the fun and freedom of seeing a daisy from many points of view. Is it a complicated structure or a white dot in a field of green? Reality can switch back and forth, considering how you view it.

Kinds of Imagery Used on Fabrics

The characteristics of stitcheries and the techniques used to make them place some limitations on the kinds of imagery that can be used successfully on fabrics—but not many. Here's a list of the types used in this book:

1. Linear	**4.** Exaggerated	**7.** Abstract
2. Flat	**5.** Shaded	**8.** Decorative
3. Realistic	**6.** Three-Dimensional	**9.** Other

1. Linear Imagery: A few lines can delineate a flower or a human shape; a buildup of many lines can show elaborate and detailed scenes of any kind. The hot wax lines of the batik flowers in Fig. 1-2 swoop into exuberant flowers while the painstakingly embroidered Chinese stitches create a controlled symbolic effect. Lines can serve many purposes, from decorating a surface to delineating a shape to filling in an entire scene. The stitcher's line is thread embroidered into designs by hand or by machine. Chapter 6 tells about embroidery techniques.

2. Flat Shapes: A solidly filled-in outline becomes a flat shape. This appears naturally in a silhouetted object. Surface detail disappears and the shape becomes one flat color. Stitchers use flat shapes for appliqué since it suits the technique so well. Janet Page-Kessler uses appliqué to create her flower studies (Fig. 1-3). She designs her pieces with a painter's eye, having studied art history and photography. Several examples of appliqué technique appear throughout this book; see chapter 7 for several ways to appliqué.

3. Realistic: This usually means showing an object or a scene the way a camera sees it. Visual artists have techniques to accomplish this: objects are shaded to imply a third dimension, muted in color to imply distance, or changed in shape and size to create perspective in pictorial space. Chapter 3 describes the various types of perspective and other techniques for achieving realistic effects. Many of the art quilts shown have used actual photographic imagery which is often reassembled in pieces. Chapter 5 tells how to use photographic materials and techniques.

4. Exaggerated: This is a way of emphasizing certain qualities. As an example, Disney characters are drawn with enormous eyes to make them childlike. Superman's bulging muscles attract teenagers. Barbie's anorexic look is considered attractive. None of these may appeal to you, yet when you draw you are emphasizing some aspects and diminishing others. Look carefully at various examples in this book to see how people exaggerated for effect. Drawings and artworks are opinions of objects and scenes; one way to express this opinion is to emphasize what matters.

5. Shaded: Shapes, whether realistic in proportion or exaggerated, can be shaded to imply a third dimension. Shading can be achieved by using darker or lighter colors embroidered, layered, or pieced into the fabric image. Janet Page-Kessler uses a gray fabric to shade her *Black and White Study* of a flower (Fig. 1-3). The gray could also imply a color change, so she gets double mileage out of this choice.

6. Three-Dimensional: Not all dimension is merely implied in stitcheries. Some is real. Quilting over puffy filler creates shadows and highlights for a more interesting surface. In Margaret Cusack's scene of the lamb and lion (Fig. 1-4), the velvet boy and woolly lamb have real depth. No additional stuffing was needed since the thick fabrics compress under the machine-sewn lines. Trapunto, quilting with added stuffing, is another way of creating bas-relief sculpture—artwork that has real dimension but is not full all around. Actual three-dimensional figures can be added to fabric designs; see chapter 9 for this.

7. Abstract: To abstract means to epitomize, summarize, or abridge. In the art world, it is a way of condensing forms. This "shorthand" angers some viewers because they find little or no easily recognizable imagery sitting on the ground where it should. They grumble phrases like "Crazy modern art" and "My kid could do that"—and their kids can abstract, as it is instinctive to simplify and epitomize scenes. A child might make a black triangle to show the secret wonders of the attic. Kids know they could add all the details, but it isn't necessary for their purposes. Almost no stitcher adds everything actually there when translating a scene into fabric. Choices in detail catch the essence of the scene.

One of my favorite abstract stitchers is B. J. Adams. In *The Remarkables*, a scene of New Zealand mountains, she pops up zigzag mountains and crumples fabric into glaciers. She says, "This piece is based on a sweeping view from a

1-3. Professional quilt designer Janet Page-Kessler says about Black and White Study, *22" x 22" (56cm x 56cm), "The piece is composed much like a painting, on the wall. Each piece contains fifty to sixty different shapes and sometimes almost as many fabrics." Photo: Artist.*

1-4. Award-winning fabric-collage artist Margaret Cusack's work usually appears as cover art on national magazines. The First Noel, *13" x 16" (33cm x 41cm), also made a fine Christmas card. Photo: Ron Breland.*

1-5. The remarkable New Zealand mountains The Remarkables, *30-1/2" x 36-1/2" (77cm x 93cm), provided imagery for fiber artist B. J. Adams. Photo: Breger and Associates, Kensington, Maryland.*

hotel room in Queenstown, New Zealand. From there one could see 'The Remarkables' mountains overlooking Lake Waikatipu in this Swiss-like mountain sanctuary. I gave myself the challenge of distilling the scene in black-and-white stripes" (Fig. 1-5). By gathers and folds, she emphasizes the natural characteristics of both fabric and earth, reminding viewers that mountains were formed of crumpled and convoluted earth but on a grander scale.

The magic of abstract art—and of all art—comes from keeping strongly in mind the ideas and emotions you want to express. The viewers will sense your meanings; well, maybe not always, but then not all art succeeds. Images may not be recognizable but the effect gives a sense of reality.

8. Decorative: Some imagery is decorative for effect. The Chinese bird and the other ethnic designs in Fig. 1-2 have been codified into decoration. The border around the bird and the flowers done in gold threads on the silk background is more symbolic of twining branches than realistic. Pushing these elements toward decorative form and away from photographic reality strengthens their symbolic effect. The decorative surroundings imply a pleasant life.

9. Other: There are many devices for representing and translating imagery into a fabric scene, but the above are the main terms referred to later. We'll get into more art terms when we deal with designing a piece in chapter 2.

Sources of Imagery

Stitchery artists have the entire world—past and present, near and distant—to use for ideas in making pictorial imagery in quilting. The following is an assortment of places to research for themes and ideas.

1. Art and Art History: Some ideas from the past were so strong and appealing that they remain influential even today. Consider the Egyptian figures carved in stone, or the embroidered battle scenes of the *Bayeux Tapestry*, or the primitive scenes in the style of Grandma Moses paintings. Picasso, like many artists, borrowed ideas and collected influences from other artists and other cultures. Images from the art world provide fascinating ways to "see" a scene. Visit art galleries or museums regularly to see what artists are up to. In addition, examine magazines, books, homes, public buildings, and even occasionally furniture stores for artists' works.

2. Nature: Nature abounds, from your windowsill to the New Zealand mountains. Suppose you want to make an animal quilt. Research can be done in several places: First, use family pets as models. Next, study less common animals at the zoo; then look for photographs in National Geographic and nature books to find realistic examples. Whenever possible, work from primary sources using the essential lines and shapes of the real animals, not artists' works that have already been translated, simplified, exaggerated, or otherwise altered. No doubt, you will also translate, simplify, and exaggerate the images, but beginning with the real thing shows through in the final result. Try it.

3. At Home: It's not necessary to leave home to find interesting imagery. The project in this chapter (see Fig. 1-1) was based on an idea as simple as a knot in a string. Many quilting designs are based on familiar household items. Do you have favorite dishes? Favorite toys? Walk through your house and note ideas. Perhaps you see a lovely dark purple eggplant in your refrigerator, along with some oranges, apples, eggs, celery, soup cans, and cookie packages. Margaret Cusack found a fine collection in her refrigerator (see the photo on the first page). There's bound to be an interesting-shaped eggbeater, a potato masher, a juicer, a soup ladle, kitchen scissors, and more in your kitchen drawer.

4. Collections: Do you happen to have six or eight different-patterned teacups in your cupboard? That's the start of a collection. Your collection need not include high-priced antiques or artworks. It can consist of whatever things you like and accumulate. Consider thimbles, plates, figurines, boxes, duck decoys, pipes, old coins, ale tankards, souvenir spoons, or tools. How about those sports or game trophies?

5. Family Albums: To use imagery with emotional ties, look through your family albums, baby books, wedding pictures, family trees, and scrapbooks. The project in chapter 5 makes use of a family photo (see Fig. 5-1). A trip down your street or through your town can provide scenes to immortalize, as many towns did in 1976 when the two-hundredth anniversary of the United States brought attention to historic scene quilts. In our town, some buildings were still standing, ready to be sketched or photographed, but for defunct favorites, like the old brick schoolhouse, sources for historical pictures were consulted, including newspaper files, old photo albums, library archives and more.

6. Books: The library holds an endless supply of ideas. Wonderful illustrations for children's books can translate sometimes directly into quilt squares. Scenes from exotic foreign lands provide fascinating architecture and gardening. Cookbooks show amazing ways to prepare and arrange foods. Scientific books show the beautiful shapes and colors of rocks and minerals, the wondrous array of sea creatures, the skies above us in all their changes of weather, and microscopic structures, to name but a few intriguing images. The Bible provided Lee Porter with imagery in his *By the Waters of Babylon* (Fig. 1-6), as it has for other artists for generations.

1-6. Lee Porter interpreted a biblical theme, the Babylonian exile, in a colorful appliquéd quilted scene called By The Waters of Babylon, *58" x 52" (145 cm x 130 cm). Photo: Mark Gulezian.*

7. Occupations: Nancy Jane Collins is a farmer and tending the chickens and the fields gives her a wealth of imagery (Fig. 1-7). She catches the flavor of farm life in the details she includes. Margaret Cusack lives and works in the city, and her work reflects different architectural space. If you see something every day at your job, the scene may lack novelty to you, but be assured that you probably know accurate details about it.

1-7. As one herself, Nancy Jane Collins knows how delighted farm folk are when the drought ends. Her wall quilt What God Has Promised, *48" x 36" (122cm x 92cm), shows this. Photo: Burge Photography; Owner: Dr. Martha Howell.*

1-8. Mary Gentry wanted to state a strong feminist point of view in her imagery so she chose the feminine medium of hand-sewn, quilted fabrics for her award-winning Quilt, about 60" x 84" (150cm x 210cm). Photo: Bill Pellitier.

8. Thoughts: Information, ideas, and opinions provide some of the strongest imagery. ABC quilts are the most obvious example of educational information. Many church wall hangings, altar cloths, and vestments show religious symbology. Mary Gentry's *Quilt* (Fig. 1-8) pictures political and social commentary. The quilt looks playful and beguiling on first inspection, with its dark rich colors and childlike frontal figures, but then you see that the tranquil calico family in the center is surrounded by the complexity, duplicity, and symbology of contemporary society. Other artists in this book express equally strong views in their pieces.

9. Purpose: The imagery you choose to incorporate into your work can have any purpose you wish: colorful, nostalgic, informative, playful, serious, political, religious, and so on. The purpose of decorative pieces can be to carry out a color scheme in a room. Political commentary pieces can express your most heartfelt feelings about ecology, population, or war. Complex combinations of forms, colors, and textures can project equally complex feelings.

10. Technique: The way stitcheries are made influences their design. Art and technique intermingle in everything people make, to one degree or another. This is no surprise since people devoting much time and attention to making their creations often decide to add embellishments. Even in periods when decoration was out of fashion, designers strove to create their plain objects artistically. Other design elements, such as proportion and scale, become important when there is little or no surface design to beguile the eye. Some quilters even now aim for such simplicity, just as many others lavish their creations with detail. As an example, Erma Martin Yost uses a variety of techniques in her stitcheries: machine embroidery, photographic images, dye painting, real objects, and more (see C-1 in the color section).

We've got a world of ideas to choose from.

USING IDEAS

Drawing Technique

Drawing is a handy skill, a process for changing a three-dimensional image into a flat design, a required step in applying imagery to fabric. It's not absolutely necessary to know how to draw to make pictorial quilts since there are so many ways to borrow imagery. However, you'll like being able to draw to implement your ideas, to organize your designs, to transfer your images, and to make your patterns.

I'm not listening if you say you can't draw. That means you quit trying in the third grade when the kid in the next seat was better at it. Or you think you must invent whatever you draw. Anyone who can write a letter can draw. To draw, you need practice in two skills: to see spatially and to make the pencil in your hand record what you see.

These are the steps to follow in drawing an object:

1. Study the object.	**4.** Look at everything.	**6.** Practice.
2. Follow the contour.	**5.** Turn it upside down.	**7.** Do "thumbnails."
3. Don't look at your drawing.		

1-9. For a subject, tie a knot in a cord and study the contours to see how it really looks. Draw what you actually see, not what you think you see.

1. Study the Object: To draw an object for use on a stitchery, first study closely the object you've chosen. Look at it long enough to see what happens. What shapes overlap other shapes? Where do the lines go? What shape are the spaces in between? (Study these in Fig. 1-9.)

2. Follow the Contour: Draw exactly what you see. This means that you will spend more time looking than drawing. Trust your brain. Already it is simplifying, telling your pencil to follow the outline to represent the shape. Artists use this technique, which is called contour drawing. Staring at the object continuously while sketching it helps settle the argument one part of your brain is having with the other. "No, no, it is not supposed to look like that," the picky side keeps saying. "But it does look like this," your eyes say. Artists override this phenomena by using the visual sides of their brains. You've got one, too, but if you use an eraser constantly you probably aren't fully in there.

3. Don't Look at Your Drawing: To see without constricting opinions, try this: Draw the object without looking at the paper. This forces you to study the outlines. Trace each bump and wiggle of the contour without thinking about how the result will look. You can look down once or twice to start a new line, but no more. You will find details you didn't know were there.

4. *Look at Everything:* Take a sketchbook with you everywhere and draw: people, furniture, trees, machines, whatever is there. One accomplished stitcher asked me for drawing lessons. Armed with her sketchbook she made contour sketches of everything, including the philodendron plant in the dentist's office. "It's not a very attractive plant," she said, but it was a wonderfully accurate portrait. Anyone could see the poor thing desperately needed nourishment as it reached its scraggly tendrils toward the window.

5. *Turn it Upside Down:* Here's another way to override your opinions of how something *should* look. If you are drawing from a photo or picture, turn it upside down so you can't tell what it is. This forces you to see the picture as lines and shapes. You'll notice the relationships of the parts, the shapes of spaces in between, the dark and light areas. This also works in scaling up patterns to reproduce what you actually see (Fig. 1-10).

6. *Practice:* Learn to trust your visual brain to guide your hand, and it will. Drawing is an instinctive ability. Your brain can recognize objects from a few lines on paper, if they are the essential lines. The more you draw, the better you'll become in putting down the most necessary details. Your drawings will have a sense of honesty about them. Once you have captured the basic form, you can translate them into stitcheries in a variety of ways.

7. *Do Thumbnails:* Make small sketches of your ideas (Fig. 1-11). Working in this size saves time, paper, and energy and allows you to try a number of views one after the other. It often provides a better overall design because it's too small to get lost in details. From a small sketch, you can see how the whole thing will look. It's usually best to scale up these small designs rather than freehand enlarge them. Proportions tend to change in freehand drawing.

Technique for Making Plans, Patterns, and Templates

A plan is the accurate overall design for your artwork and serves for the placement of the pieces as well as the shape of the pattern pieces. Trace patterns or templates from this master plan or use it for cutting or stitching through. You may need to make extra copies.

Patterns are guides for cutting out or sewing pieces. They include seam allowances, when necessary, and other notations for construction. They can be made of paper, fabric, or materials of heavier weight.

Templates are patterns without seam allowances. They are often made of stiff material to withstand the tracing of seam lines around them.

Plans, patterns, and templates for flat pictorial quilting can be made directly from a drawing or other imagery because they do not need to have three-dimensional shape designed in, as clothing patterns must. Even so, the way the piece is constructed does affect the pattern. For instance, hand-sewn appliqué pieces will need to have seam allowances all around the edges for hemming and so must not be too complicated to be successfully hemmed.

1. To make a plan of a pattern, select white or light-colored paper in medium to light weight. The paper should be flexible enough to fold for future use and firm enough for pinning through. Choose paper you can draw on to record directions (such as "cut 2"), seam allowances, grain line, and surface designs to be imprinted on the fabric face.

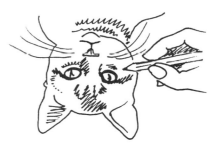

1-10. *If the idea of reproducing a drawing daunts you, turn it upside down to see it simply as lines and shapes instead of imagery.*

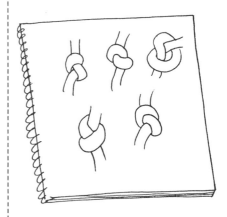

1-11. *Try drawing several views in small sketches, called thumbnails, to arrive at the most usable image. Scale this up to size to keep the spontaneity of the drawing.*

2. For a template, choose plastic or cardboard for stability in tracing. Templates are used for tracing multiple pieces, as in pieced quilts, or for tracing seam lines on the reverse side to keep quilt blocks squared. Templates for English piecing are made of paper and sewn into the piecing (see the chapter 3 project for this).

3. Consider the construction requirements when making a plan and designing patterns. The design of the *Knot Kakimono* consists of a central pictorial unit surrounded by framing in plain and printed fabrics. Having a smaller central unit or multiple smaller units means less volume to wrestle through the sewing machine in order to stitch the imagery. Study your plan to determine what pieces overlap lower ones so construction can be simplified.

4. Once you've settled on the design draw a full-sized plan on the paper. (For transferring and scaling-up techniques, see chapter 5.) Use a pencil or permanent pen and make narrow-width seam lines. Be careful of crayon or water-base pens that might smear.

5. Trace pattern pieces from your plan, adding seam allowances as needed. Quilting magazines and fabric stores sell various devices for adding an even 1/4" or wider seam allowance.

6. Trace around a template pattern on the reverse side of the fabric and don't rely on seam allowance widths. A template of the full pattern piece provides a more accurate stitch or folding line. You can work from templates and add seam allowances in the cutting. Your best bet is to make both a pattern and a template for multiple or complex pieces.

7. Some plans need to be duplicated because they are destroyed in the construction process, as is the one below. Some need to be reversed by tracing on the back side. Early on, I worked with no patterns or with casual ones later thrown away, but now I save them all in a file drawer in Zip-lock bags so I can refer to them as needed. More information on patterns appears throughout this book.

In each chapter, special projects give techniques to allow hands-on experience. Within the *Knot Kakimono* are directions for a type of machine appliqué, adding trapunto, satin-stitch outlining, and assembling a scroll.

If you don't want to plow through all those dimensions and details in the projects to locate various techniques, skim the headings until you come to the phrase "Technique for————" and read those sections. In this first project, as in some others, a technique is used before a chapter fully explains it. If necessary, consult the specific chapter that deals with this issue first: for example, read about appliqué in chapter 7.

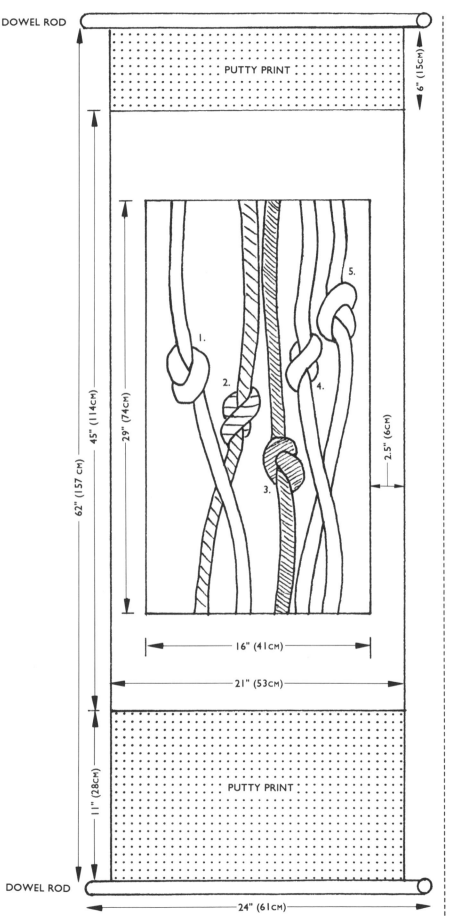

DOWEL ROD

PUTTY PRINT

6" (15cm)

62" (157 CM)

45" (114CM)

29" (74CM)

2.5" (6CM)

ROPE 1. – METALLIC PRINT

ROPE 2. – PEACH

ROPE 3. – MULTI-COLOR
              STRIPE

ROPE 4. – GOLD/SILVER
              BROCADE

ROPE 5. – BROWN

16" (41CM)

21" (53CM)

11" (28CM)

PUTTY PRINT

DOWEL ROD

24" (61CM)

1-12. The plan and patterns for Knot Kakimono. Scale this up to size (see chapter 5 for this procedure).

Victorville Branch Library
15011 Circle Drive
Victorville, CA 92392

PROJECT: SIMPLE IMAGES, *KNOT KAKIMONO*
(Fig. 1-12; see also Fig. 1-1 and C-2)

Overview: This Japanese-style wall hanging shows uncomplicated imagery that you might find anywhere. It is made by sewing through the reversed paper pattern from the back to provide guidelines and then sewn through again on these lines and the appliqué pieces to anchor them. Stuffed appliqué pieces (the knots) are added to the front.

Theme: This wall hanging incorporates two main ideas: first, that a simple granny knot is an intriguing shape and, next, that the traditional Japanese kakimono scroll provides a fine format.

Techniques: (1) Stacked appliqué sewn through the pattern plan; (2) added trapunto shapes; (3) satin-stitch outlining; and (4) assembling a scroll.

Size: 24" x 62" (61cm x 157cm) includes 1" x 24" (61cm) rods.

Colors: Ropes: peach, brown, metallic, striped (orange, blue, gold, and maroon), and gray; background: warm off-white; frame: putty and black on putty print; rods: dark brown.

Note: If the exact colors listed are not available, carefully relate the colors you choose to each other. Buy extra fabric for safety margins. The following measurements include seam allowances.

MATERIALS

Note: Fabrics used in this were slippery and frayed so a trim-later machine appliqué technique was used.

Design panel: Background: 17" x 30" (43cm x 76cm) off-white lustrous rayon or polyester (damask-woven in rose pattern or what suits).

Knot/ropes (from left): Cut five pieces of fabric 6" x 34" (15cm x 86cm). Rope One: brown metallic tapestry weave; Rope Two: peach taffeta; Rope Three: woven stripe (orange, blue, gold, maroon); Rope Four: white, gold, and silver metallic tapestry; Rope Five: brown satin.

Frame front and backing: One piece 22" x 46" (56cm x 117cm) and one piece 22" x 63" (56cm x 160cm) taupe linenlike fabric.

Frame top and bottom panels: 7" x 22" (18cm x 56cm) and 12" x 22" (30.5cm x 56cm) black and putty print cotton fabric.

Lining: 16" x 29" (41cm x 74cm) and 21" x 62" (53cm x 157cm) canvas-weight cotton. Use fusible webbing backing as desired.

Threads: Machine embroidery thread in orange, brown, dark gray, blue-gray, and white; regular putty sewing thread.

Rods: Two 1" (2.5mm) wooden dowels 24" (61cm) long, painted dark brown.

Tools and supplies: Zigzag sewing machine, special purpose embroidery foot, staple gun, sewing machine, sharp scissors, pins, and paint.

PROCEDURE

Technique for Machine Appliqué with Untrimmed Layers

Note: For more details on this process, read chapter 7 on appliqué first, if needed.

1 Make a paper plan the full size of the center panel. (This plan/pattern is ruined in the sewing.) Trace on the reverse side of the paper pattern and number the ropes as to the pattern.

2 Make a second identical plan. Label the colors of the knots. Cut out the knots on the seam lines, saving the pattern as a placement guide. Number the ropes.

3 Baste the background fabric to the lining. Pin the reversed plan to the lining and straight-stitch all the lines through the plan with contrasting thread to transfer the guidelines to the center panel front. Leave the paper plan on the lining to stabilize during satin-stitching.

4 Straight-stitch orange diagonal lines 3/4" (2cm) apart on the peach fabric to indicate rope twist. Cut off 4" x 6" (10cm x 15cm) for the knot. Place the peach fabric so it covers the Rope Two stitch lines on the center panel front and pin outside the lines (Fig. 1- 13). Ropes One and Five are sewn first because other ropes overlap them.

5 Set your machine for a narrow zigzag. From the back, sew over Rope Two lines following the straight-stitch lines except for the knot. From the front, trim away the excess fabric close to the stitch line.

6 Repeat steps 4 and 5 for Rope Five. Trim away where it passes under the lighter rope so it will not shadow through. (Do this where one color or texture shadows through another.)

7 Repeat steps 4 and 5 for the other three ropes, not stitching where the ropes cross.

Technique for Adding Trapunto

Note: For more details on trapunto, see chapter 9.

1 Place wads of stuffing (about 1" [2.5cm] thick uncompressed) within the knot guidelines, slightly overlapping lines.

2 Cover these with matching knot fabrics. Arrange the striped knot and the orange diagonal line on the peach knot according to the pattern. Pin knot fabrics in place, mounded over the stuffing avoiding wrinkles around the edges (Fig. 1-14).

3 Pin the pattern with cutout knots over the panel as a template for stitching. Sew around each knot at the seam line with a narrow zigzag stitch. Carefully trim away excess fabric as close to the zigzag stitch line as possible. Be careful not to cut the backing fabric or the basting stitches.

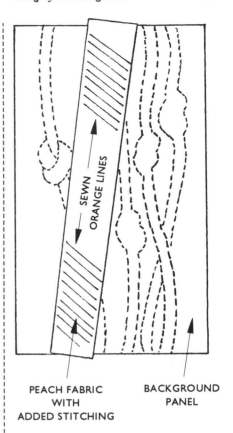

PEACH FABRIC WITH ADDED STITCHING   BACKGROUND PANEL

1-13. To appliqué the knot/rope fabric on, place the appropriate-colored fabric over the pattern lines stitched through the pattern from the back onto the background fabric.

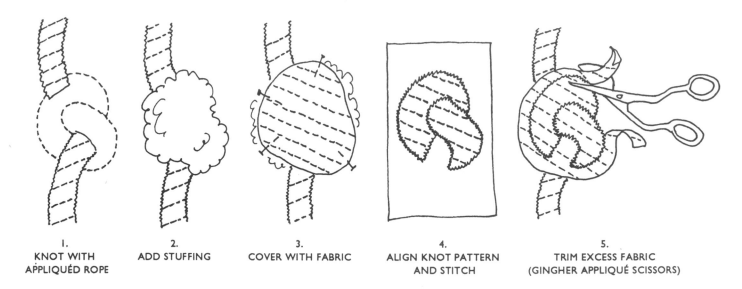

1.	2.	3.	4.	5.
KNOT WITH APPLIQUÉD ROPE	ADD STUFFING	COVER WITH FABRIC	ALIGN KNOT PATTERN AND STITCH	TRIM EXCESS FABRIC (GINGHER APPLIQUÉ SCISSORS)

1-14. For padded knots, put a puff of stuffing on the knot. Cover this with fabric. Align the knot pattern as a guide to machine-stitch the padded knot. After stitching, trim excess fabric away.

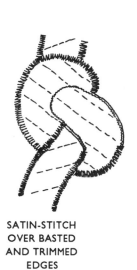

SATIN-STITCH
OVER BASTED
AND TRIMMED
EDGES

OVER LAP

1-15. Satin-stitch the appliqué edges over the basted and trimmed edges. Satin-stitch the topmost shape last to cover stitching endings neatly.

Technique for Outline Satin-Stitch Appliqué

Note: See chapter 6 for more information on machine embroidery.

1 Set your machine to a wider zigzag and shorter stitch length for a satin-stitch about 3/16" wide (5mm). Use a special-purpose embroidery presser foot with space on the bottom for clearing the satin-stitching. Sew a test piece to adjust it. Be sure the satin-stitch row is wide enough to cover the trimmed appliqué fabric and is solid enough to hide the basting.

Note: The canvas-weight lining stabilizes the background against the pull of the zigzag machine stitching and keeps the stitchery flat.

2 On Rope Two, use orange thread to satin-stitch in this order: (1) the peach-colored rope outline; (2) the two smaller knot sections; and (3) the crossover part of the knot. Stitching in this order gives the neatest finished effect where two stitch lines meet (Fig. 1-15).

3 Outline the brown tapestry Rope/Knot One and brown Rope/Knot Five with a darker brown thread. Outline the striped Rope/Knot Three with blue-gray, and the silver/gold tapestry Rope/Knot Four with dark gray, each in the order given.

Assembling the Scroll (Fig. 1-16)

1 Turn a 1/2" (12mm) hem on the edges of the completed design panel. Place and pin it accurately on the taupe-colored framing fabric.

2 Straight-stitch the hemmed panel in place and then satin-stitch over this using a white thread.

3 Refer to the diagram (see Fig. 1-12) to measure and pencil mark seam lines on the reverse side of the taupe and printed framing fabrics. Align the taupe and printed framing fabrics face-to-face, pin through the stitch line to match seam lines, and straight-stitch the seam.

4 Align the finished top with the backing and stitch around the edges, leaving a 6" (15cm) opening to turn. Clip corners, turn, and press. Hand sew the opening closed.

5 Paint the dowel rods dark brown or an appropriate color and let dry.

6 Staple the scroll to the dowel rods. Attach a decorative cord to the top rod to hang.

1-16. To assemble the scroll, top-stitch the knot/rope panel to the backing. Seam on the printed fabric ends. Sew the front and back together, turn, and clip corners and grade seam allowances. Staple to a painted dowel rod to complete.

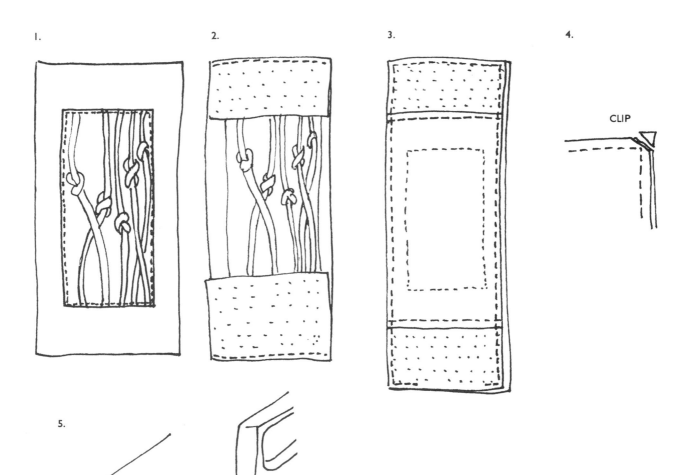

2-1. *The process for designing a quilt like Family Teapot Quilt, 54" x 70" (137cm x 179cm) is covered in the project section at the end of chapter 2. Photo: Lori Tennent.*

DESIGN: ARRANGING ELEMENTS

Chapter Two

"What shall I make?"

Y ou, like every artist, ask yourself this question because your creative juices are running high. You want to make something lasting; something others can enjoy. Further, you want a project interesting enough to engage your brain, challenging enough to tax your skills, and successful enough to bring pleasure in the accomplishment. Making a picture quilt can fill all these needs and more.

This chapter details the creation of a pictorial quilt or other stitchery, from the design decisions through arranging the component parts to instructions for making the quilt shown (Fig. 2-1).

A good first step is to give yourself a detailed assignment. To begin, you need not have all the details in mind; they'll surface as you proceed. My assignment to myself for this chapter was to think of an idea for a pictorial quilt in order to show the steps in creating it. "Pick a theme that's simple but appealing," I told myself. "Use an idea that can be done in a variety of ways and yet one that isn't going to take forever to make. Choose something I really like and want to have when it's done since I'm going to spend hours and hours doing it."

Assigning yourself a project takes it out of the daydream category and puts you on the road to making it real. In chapter 1, B. J. Adams mentioned gazing out her window, awestruck by the scenery of New Zealand. Eager to save those feelings and share them with others, she said, "I gave myself the challenge of distilling the scene."

If there's a terrific view you've always wanted to enshrine, use that as your assignment. If you have an exquisite fabric on hand or if you crave something with beautiful colors for your house, use this as a springboard to begin. Keep in mind that you don't want a project so big it never gets done, nor so tedious to make that you hate it before completion. Also, it can't be so precious that nobody can touch it. Considering these aspects of your assignment helps to make decisions about how to proceed.

MAKING IT REAL

Design Checklist

Normally, you would make these decisions in your head, but for now, sit down with a notebook or sketchpad to think on paper. Here's a list of questions to ask yourself that will diagram your project. Leave space on your list for adding notes.

1. What do I want to make?
2. How will it be used?
3. What is the idea behind it?
4. What kind of imagery do I plan to use?
5. How do I plan to make it?
6. What size or shape should it be?
7. What colors will be right for it?
8. What materials would look and work best?
9. Other choices.

Planning the Project

Begin by jotting down answers to these questions or begin by making sketches of ideas you'd like to try. Neatness doesn't count at this point nor does it matter whether you think in images or words. The point is to stimulate your brain.

Start with any question you can answer, regardless of its order on the list. Answer one question and you have begun to outline your assigned project since each decision affects the others. For example, deciding on a theme affects the colors, colors affect fabric choices, fabrics and size affect cost and time, and so on. If you are inventing the piece as you go, you probably can't decide everything first, however the more decisions you can make before beginning the fewer problems you'll meet later. Some ideas follow to help you in considering these questions.

1. What Do I Want to Make? The answer to this question is your assignment. Do you need a quilt for your bed? Do you want to try a certain technique? Have you a wonderful idea for a theme? Do you need a piece for an exhibition? Do you want to begin selling your work? Do you have opinions you feel you must impart to the world? Your aim in making something could be practical or aesthetic or any combination of the above.

Don't be surprised if you can't seem to get started on a piece until it seems important. If you have the luxury of time—meaning you aren't making quilts for cash or accepting specific commissions—wait until a piece demands to be done. Being guided by a "sense of mission" helps make impelling works. The same feelings that urge you to make the piece will help you make design decisions, such as nostalgic colors, sensuous textures, or serious imagery. Trust this emotional guidance and go with it. The result will be a stronger piece.

Merrill Mason describes her motivation this way: "I want my work to reflect and illuminate my times and the world I live in. I use photographic constructions [as she calls her fiber pieces] to consider social and political issues by contrasting the conventional associations of stitched cloth—beauty, security and domesticity—with unlikely provocative content, and by treating ugliness as though it were beautiful" (Fig. 2-2).

2. How Will It Be Used? Sometimes the purpose of the piece suggests the format. Merrill Mason starts with a strongly held idea, in this case, anger at toxic dump sites. Your aim might be more domestic; a king-size quilt would look great in the master bedroom. Purpose covers a lot of ground. It can include expression, utility, decoration, gift-giving, exhibition, and more.

2-2. *"My work combines photography with the traditional woman's art forms of pieced cloth and embroidery, aiming to create lush, seductive images out of the industrial landscape," artist Merrill Mason of Art Quilt Network–New York says of Scrap Thatch, 65" x 91" (165cm x 231cm). The phototransfer quilt blocks, in this case with no sashing, are machine pieced, machine and hand embroidered, and machine appliquéd. Photo: Erik Landsberg.*

Purpose can focus your energies as you envision how wonderful your creation is going to look or how suitable it will be when it is done. It also helps define the project and answer other questions. What size must it be to fit a bed or qualify for an exhibition? What materials must be used for washability? Can you finish it before the anniversary party?

A purpose that is too restricting can be intimidating. Making a king-size quilt is such a cumbersome project that only the most stalwart should take it on. Statements about abortion or starvation may be too strong for the living room. Don't let the purpose dictate too many rules and ruin your enthusiasm.

3. *What Is the Idea Behind It?* Pictorial art usually has a theme or story behind it that gives a reason for the images to appear as they do. Sometimes, an artist has a million of these ideas stored up waiting to be done; sometimes, there are none. For this chapter I sat at my desk searching for a theme idea to illustrate the design process.

"Easy," I told myself, staring at the blank paper. Faint images flitted through my head like jungle animals approaching the watering hole. These images vanished, spooked by a hunter, when I tried to catch them. This state of mind called for a cup of tea. My everyday teapot with blue designs would do fine; no need to risk the good china one.

One way to make something happen is to keep a sketch book at hand and note ideas in it as they come. Ideas beget ideas. To save ideas, put anything in your sketchbook that captures the essence: your own sketches, a notation saying what is intended, clippings from magazines or other sources, color ideas, whatever. These drawings need not be of museum quality, only adequate to save the idea until you have time to explore it later. I sketched my teapot since it was sitting there keeping the tea warm.

Sometimes, no idea is sitting there waiting. In this case, scan through your sketchbook to see what catches your interest. Nothing? Leaf through other books, ramble through the mall, go to an art gallery, walk in the woods, or sort through the scrap basket for inspiring pieces of fabric. Take time to examine the world around you with questing eyes. Examples in chapter 1 showed how people found ideas for their creations usually quite close to home.

Traditional art forms spare the stitcher the need to start from scratch. How and what to make are, in a large part, answered if nearly all quilts in a society are made in a similar way. In our country, though, there are hundreds of traditional patchwork or appliqué designs to choose from. A quilter need only decide on the size and color to begin. Yet pictorial quilters quite often want to make their own choices and create something new. They want to say something.

I'm still thinking . . . and my teapot is still holding the heat well, better than the pewter pot we got in Holland on our first overseas trip. I haven't actually tried making tea in the curious ceramic teapot found in China that is covered with a tightly woven reed jacket. Nor in the antique pewter one that's been in the Hall family since 1735—and looks it! Teapots! That's my theme sitting right in front of me: my life as annotated by acquiring teapots. I rapidly warm to the idea, planning to include my mother's best teapot to commemorate the heart-to-hearts we had over tea and the elegant antique silver one my daughter gave me for Christmas, knowing we'll share it.

Brown

white
Black

pewter

Pewter

natural beige
Bronze Blue
Accents

Bamboo.
Embroidery

Colors

white.
blue designs

white

silver

pewter

Kid's teapot

2-3. *A page from the author's sketch book shows teapots from her informal collection. What collections might you have around the house for quilt imagery?*

4. What Kind of Imagery Do I Plan to Use? Once you choose a theme, the next step is to decide how to handle it. Excited by my theme idea, I ran around the house ferreting out the teapots on shelves and in cupboards and then sketching them (Fig. 2-3). Can it be possible that I have thirteen teapots, more if the grandchildren's toy ones are counted? Looking at my sketches, I wonder which one teapot is the most appealing. Perhaps it should be featured in a scene with a cup and saucer . . . a plate with cookies . . . the table it is sitting on. The picture begins to create itself, but it doesn't quite say what I wish. I want to use them all.

Recalling the first chapter on kinds of imagery stirs my brain. How about outline drawings for the teapots? Or flat shapes? Do I want realism or exaggeration of the shapes? Should I shade them in someway, or actually make them three-dimensional? I finally decide yes to about half of the above. (Artists like deciding yes to questions.) Since I've opted for realism, I can eliminate thinking about what style I might choose, such as country or Art Deco.

Marilyn Price uses standard quilting techniques of patchwork and quilted layers but accomplishes an Art Deco effect in her wall hanging by using design devices of this era: diagonal steps and architecturally rounded panels (see C-3 in the color section). These forms are being rediscovered by architects, designers, and others these days.

On my page of sketches, I had made small pots larger and large ones smaller. Opting for realism requires making objects in correct proportion to one another, so I decided to trace the teapot outlines as a quick way of making these round objects flat. (See chapter 5 on transferring images for how to do this.)

5. How Do I Plan to Make It? Decisions already made will reduce the time required to work out the rest of the details. I especially like machine appliqué to apply flat shapes to fabric, so that takes care of technique. If I were working in resist dyes or photo transfer techniques, I might as easily have selected one of those techniques to use. Lori Bolt Hassled works in screen printing and machine embroidery. Lori also likes hearts and commonly incorporates all three in her pillows which sell readily at street fairs (Fig. 2-4). The goal is to fit the technique to the imagery or the other way around depending on the way you work.

6. What Size or Shape Should It Be? Function, location, and technique all influence the size and shape. For example, hand embroidery provides exquisite details but making a large quilt this way could take forever. Conversely, appliqué shapes can add color quickly. The time it takes to make the piece must be taken into consideration, so choose the size project you can handle.

What separates creative people from others is that they keep picturing the finished piece more than they consider the effort to accomplish it. Dreamers, however, rarely consider the details of construction. Doers must. A lovely idea may be too complicated and time consuming. However, the size can be reduced to units such as quilt blocks or strips, and worked on bit by bit.

One marvelous thing about quilts is that they can be as large as paintings yet still roll or fold to put away. Even so, don't make your display quilt taller than your wall. A quilt seven feet tall fills an eight foot wall when you consider the

2-4. Lori Bolt Hassled used grids, from a tiny print background to the larger squares on her screen-printed pillows and played with heart imagery. The pillows measure about 16" to 18" (40.5cm to 45cm) square.

2-5. The traditional log cabin quilt block design creates different overall patterns depending on the arrangement of the dark and light halves of the blocks (right).

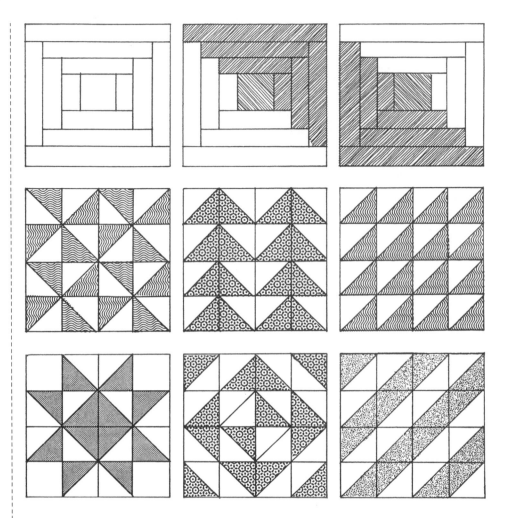

hanging rod and floor clearance. Older quilts were rarely large; few but kings had king-size beds when quilting got its start.

7. *What Colors Will Be Right for It?* Color choice is tied to imagery, the materials used, and the techniques of representation or construction employed. Having opted for realism, I aimed to find fabrics as close in color and texture to the real pots as possible. I used metallics for the silver and newer pewter pots yet a mousy-colored taupe satin looked best for the old one. Where I could not match colors, I combined several close ones to give a dimensional effect, and then embellished them with various colored threads to add more color touches.

To get a complete look at the piece in the color planning stage, I laid it out on the floor. This allowed me to view it overall for balance or directional flow. Colors (pieces of cloth) can be switched back and forth at this stage until a harmonious effect is achieved. Colors always relate to one another, so changing one may change them all; (see chapter 8 on color).

8. *What Materials Would Look and Work Best?* My trove of stored fabric holds some pieces I may never find a use for, but I must save each one just in case I ever do. In searching for the right colors for each teapot, and hoping to avoid yet another trip to the fabric store, I discovered a collection of old linens.

Many of these fabrics had seen use as tablecloths, some were the right vintage for a particular pot, and others served ideally to carry out the mood of the piece. The fabrics carried as much nostalgia for remembered times and places in my past as did the pots themselves.

Considering fabrics can inspire ideas. Touching the fabrics helps visualize the form they could take. Light bounces off of or is absorbed by fabrics in different ways. Evenly placed hand-stitching can give a sculptured rhythm to the fabric; for more about choice of materials, see chapter 9.

9. Other Choices: There are assorted other decisions to make about your projects. Not all need be made at the beginning. Estimating construction time matters only if you are pricing a piece for sale, have limited time, or must meet a deadline. Also, care of the finished piece may be a factor. Where it will be hung can affect the design decisions. Will it be exposed to damaging daylight or pollution? A wall hanging I made for a restaurant eventually became impregnated with airborne steak fat. Fortunately, drycleaning saved it.

Like everything else, materials rise in price continually. This could be a major issue if you are trying to survive as a producing craftsperson. Quilt prices have not caught up with the rest of the art market, according to the *Wall Street Journal* and all the quilt makers I know. Further, quilted pieces take longer to create than most art forms.

Which brings up the aesthetics of your work. You do not need to aim for exhibition quality work but do keep your standards high. The adage "If it's worth doing, it's worth doing well" certainly applies to quilting. Aim for harmony of the parts, invention in color, skill in technique, and seriousness of purpose even in playful pieces.

Arranging Component Parts

Here's where your artist's eye comes in. Remember those pictures taken with your first camera. . . people's faces centered, bodies cut off at hip level, and lots of sky? It's time to see differently. Forget that those people are Aunt Ruth and Uncle Joe and see them in terms of shadows and highlights, color contrasts, balance of spaces, and arrangement of forms.

1. Design Elements: Once you've chosen the imagery, you need to determine how to place it. As you compose a piece, shift your mind away from what the scene represents and into seeing it as shapes, lines, and colors. Do the parts of your scene balance? Symmetrical balance means everything on one side has a match on the other. Asymmetrical balance means a dark color may be balanced by a light one or a plain area by an intricately detailed one. Is there visual movement: around in a circle, in an S curve, diagonally? Does repetition of the forms create a rhythm or does variation in forms create emphasis? You are in charge here, guiding the viewer's eye around your scene.

2. Units: Traditionally, quilts are made in repeated units. This format provides separate blocks of a handy size for hand sewing or fitting it into the sewing machine. In addition, repeating the unit over and over creates a rhythm like the beat in music. A single musical note may not be effective by itself but a pattern of them makes a song. The most common format for quilts is a unit repeated in a grid.

3. Overall Scene: At other times, a single unit is used. Merrill Mason in *Scrap Thatch* (see Fig. 2-2) shows a scrap heap in which the discarded junk becomes a texture of repeated shapes. This photographic fabric piece treats a scene as design. Sometimes, the subject is treated as a scene and then pictorial space is a factor, but that comes in chapter 3. For now the problem is arranging units.

4. Interlocking Patterns: An overall grid of units or blocks creates a pattern of its own. A good example of this is the log cabin quilt. When the logs in the unit are laid in contrasting dark and light, a stair-step diagonal is formed. When the blocks are placed in a grid as is, the overall effect is one of stacked triangles (Fig. 2-5). Still within the grid, start turning the block to see what you get: stars, diagonals, diamonds, or zigzags.

VARIATIONS ON PATTERNS: NETWORKS

The primary unit can be arranged or varied in shape in several ways and still interlock perfectly with the next (Fig. 2-6). This is called a network. Networks include these basic patterns:

1. Grid	*3.* Half-drop brick	*5.* Triangles	*7.* Hexagon
2. Brick	*4.* Diamond	*6.* Scales	*8.* Ogee

Of course, you've seen grid quilts, but does anybody use other networks? Consider Marilyn Price, who especially likes trying variations on traditional quilt forms. In *Textile* (see C-3 in the color section) she uses the basic grid but makes it diagonal. She uses curved shapes to soften the grid effect and contrasts blocks of flat color with small photographic scenes.

In a textile mural for St. Catherine's Hospital in East Chicago, Indiana, she uses the half-drop brick design and alternates three different unit designs. The frame is composed of a variety of smaller blocks in rows (see C-4 in the color section). This one's imagery is intriguing enough so that only later do you see the underlying network structure—just as she intended!

Tafi Brown, in her piece *Rockingham Raising: Come Along* for the Georgia Power and Light Company (Fig. 2-7), uses photographic imagery for her basic units, then prints them in reverse to create a rhythmic larger unit. Rather than a grid, she arranges these in framing rows. Here the architectural structure intentionally shows through since they are raising a building, and only next do you make out the figures on the blocks.

2- 6. The most common interlocking patterns used by quilters (and other designers) are: the grid, the brick, the half-drop brick, the diamond, the triangle, the scale, the hexagon, and the ogee. Each single unit meshes perfectly with identical units.

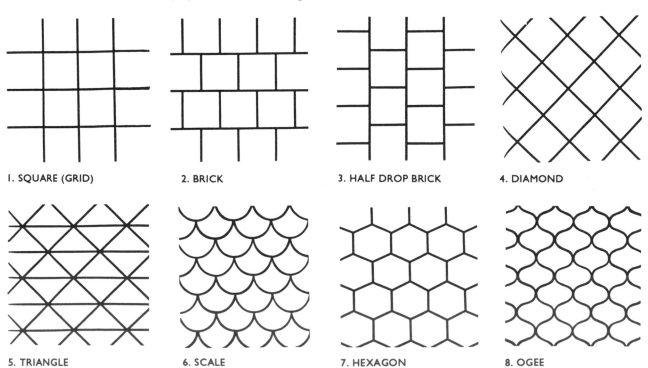

I. SQUARE (GRID)	2. BRICK	3. HALF DROP BRICK	4. DIAMOND
5. TRIANGLE	6. SCALE	7. HEXAGON	8. OGEE

By chance, Joyce Marquess Carey came across a collection of fabric squares showing Communist imagery. Her piece, *Red Square* (see C-5 in the color section) makes good use of them. In geometric precision, she meshed Joseph Stalin's and Mao Tse-Tung's portraits, done on approximately 6" (15cm) squares with smaller red squares (a clever visual pun).

Technique for Manipulating Design Units

Pictures in the mind are fleeting, so getting them down on paper helps to see and keep them. Manipulating these images into various patterns shows a variety of effects without having to make a major project to see what works.

1. To manipulate units assemble these materials:

- a pad of tracing paper or a stack of inexpensive copy paper
- several sheets of colored paper
- soft pencil, crayon, or pen
- scissors or paper cutter
- glue stick

2-7. *Tafi Brown prints on fabric quilt blocks by cyanotype, a light sensitive process used mainly for blue-printing plans. In Rockingham Raising: Come Along she flipped her photographic images of loggers for a rhythmic effect and pieced them into gridwork frames around a central unit.*

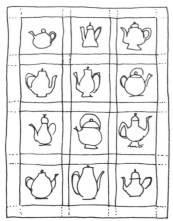   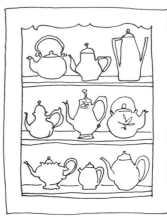

2-8. Identical or varied units, such as a teapot shape, can be arranged in endless ways to create a larger design. These are some of the ideas that were tried for the teapot quilt before settling on the traditional grid (See Fig. 2-9).

Note: For even quicker results, use a rubber stamp and/or a photocopier.

2. Working small, draw or trace the image you'd like to use. You can use the same image repeated over and over or a variety of similar-sized units as in Fig. 2-3, showing my sketch of thirteen teapots.

3. Clip apart the sketches of images into individual units, trace twelve or more copies, or make photocopies of your image. Cut out the images, in squares or around the outline of the image.

4. Arrange the images on the colored paper in various networks, in a grid, in rows, in a circle, in a frame, or whatever delights your eye. Now is the time to try all the arrangements you can imagine, when it can be done instantly. Try some you can't imagine, including gently blowing on the arrangement for a random effect.

5. Just as Marilyn Price and Tafi Brown do, you can try anything, such as cutting the colored sheets in strips, squares, network shapes, or random shapes. Arrange this new assortment with your images in various designs, regular or random in placement.

6. When you come up with a design you really like, glue or paste the images on the paper just as they are. Or do this: clear-tape the images in place, photocopy the result, save this copy, and re-use the images to create yet another study. Fig. 2-8 shows some of the designs I tried in designing the teapot quilt.

Technique for Designing Full Size

Most likely, you will need to keep making design changes all along, no matter how well you planned your project. You'll want to adjust colors, change difficult fabrics, accent parts, redo messes or whatever is needed for best results. Accept that this is part of the process of designing. I like working directly, laying out the fabrics on the floor. This allows for planning the entire piece, for coordinating the colors, and for switching fabrics at will until the overall harmonizes. Next I pin the pieces up on my portable pinning wall for a better view. (See chapter 4 for how to make one for yourself.)

Want to know my advice on coping with design problems? Get a rocking chair, pour yourself a cup of tea, and simply stare at the piece until a solution comes. This is why it is difficult to describe how long you sat pondering when people ask how long it takes to make an artwork.

2-9. *The overall pattern for the Family Teapot Quilt. Scale up to size and use the fabrics listed or select your own fabrics and colors to make this. As an alternative, choose imagery of your own for a quilt unit.*

PROJECT: MULTIPLE UNITS, *FAMILY TEAPOT QUILT*
(Fig. 2-9; and see C-6 in the color section)

Overview: My teapots or your figurine collection can serve as design elements for a picture quilt. This quilt starts with twelve gray background blocks to which various background fabrics are added, sometimes covering the block completely. Teapot shapes backed with fusible webbing are appliquéd on the blocks. The blocks and sashing are pieced together—with added narrow ribbon sewn around some blocks where needed as accent—and then assembled in layers to make the quilt. It's made envelope style, with a finished edge and a rod pocket for hanging to display.

Theme: Portraits of favorite teapots sit on table linens, actual or typical of the teapot's era and style.

Techniques: (1) Fused fabric machine appliqué; (2) template-drawn stitch lines; (3) quilt layers assembled envelope style, and (4) making a rod pocket.

Size: Overall quilt size: 54-1/2" x 70-1/4" (139cm x 179cm); block size: 13-1/2" (34cm) square; sashings 2-1/4" (6cm) wide, border 2-1/2" (6.5cm) wide.

Colors: Colors range from light pastels to muted dark colors, highlighted with metallic or other lustrous fabrics. Actual colors are listed, but you may find these aren't available or you wish to use others. In either case, it is more important that all colors relate to each other than that they be accurate.

MATERIALS

Note: Fabrics were chosen that provided the right color and texture resulting in a non-washable display quilt. If you want a usable quilt, switch to polycottons and wash all fabrics first.

Backing and border: 4 yards (366cm) striped-patterned fabric; sashing and frame: 1-2/3 yards (152cm) eggshell polycotton, 1-2/3 yards (152cm) lace or eyelet; background blocks: 1-2/3 yards (152cm) of gray polycotton.

Block fabrics *(numbered from upper left):*

  1. For the first row, 9" (23cm) square white sateen teapot, gray/pink/green chintz print 6" x 14" (15cm x 36cm): the exposed gray background fabric area is 14-1/2" x 8-1/2" (37cm x 22cm); a 56" pink 1/4" (6mm) wide ribbon.

  2. Silver-metallic fabric 9" x 10" (23cm x 26cm), ecru lace overlaying a rose-print fabric 9" x 14-1/2" (23cm x 37cm), golden-brown satin 6" x 14-1/2" (15cm x 37cm), 10-1/2" (27cm) round lace doily.

  3. Light blue metallic fabric 9" x 9" (23cm x 23cm), blue and white grid 9" x 14-1/2" (23cm x 37cm), Swiss embroidered table linen (or hand towel) 6" x 14-1/2" (15cm x 37cm) pieced together to center design; accent ribbon: 56" (142cm) blue 1/4" (6mm) wide.

  4. For the second row, eggshell 6" x 9" (15cm x 23cm), blue print 5" x 14-1/2" (13cm x 37cm), lace-edged handkerchief over exposed gray background.

  5. Taupe satin 9" x 9" (23cm x 23cm), assorted laces and crocheted placemat; accent ribbon: 56" (142cm) black 1/4" (6mm) wide.

  6. White 9" x 9" (23cm x 23cm), tan and black flower print hemmed to 7" x 14-1/2" (18cm x 37cm) (place hem of print 4-1/2" [11.5cm] from top).

7. For the third row, golden brown 9" x 9" (23cm x 23cm), blue/green 6-1/2" x 14-1/2" (15cm x 37cm), two Chinese appliquéd hand towels cut to center the designs; accent ribbon: 56" (142cm) pink 1/4" (6mm) wide.

8. Dark brown 9" x 9" (23cm x 23cm) plus golden brown 3" x 5" (7.5cm x 12.5cm) and maroon 4" x 5" (10cm x 12.5cm) appliqué highlights, blue/mauve/gray woven fabric 6-1/2" x 14-1/2" (16.5cm x 37cm), taupe and gray random dot print 8" x 14-1/2" (20.5cm x 37cm).

9. Light gray 9" x 9" (23cm x 23cm), 5" x 5" (12.5cm x 12.5cm) golden brown mug and appliqué shading, rust color 6-1/2" x 14-1/2" (16.5cm x 37cm), eggshell leno weave napkin; accent ribbon: 56" (142cm) mauve 1/4" (6mm) wide.

10. For the fourth row, silver metallic 9" x 10" (23cm x 25.5cm), dark green hand-screen print 10-1/2" x 14-1/2" (26.5cm x 37cm), white and blue-green stripes 3-1/2" x 14-1/2" (9cm x 37cm).

11. Eggshell polished cotton 9" x 9" (23cm x 23cm) plus cream accents 2" x 6" (5cm x 15cm), pink and peach print 14-1/2" (37cm) square, 16" (40.5cm) round doily with crocheted edging; accent ribbon: 56" (142cm) pink 1/4" (6.5mm) wide.

12. White 9" x 9" (23cm x 23cm) and gray 9" x 9" (23cm x 23cm) for pots, rose print 10-1/2" x 14-1/2" (26.5cm x 37cm), pink 3-1/2" x 14-1/2" (9cm x 37cm).

Filler: One batt 55" x 72" (140cm x 183cm) or nearest size fiberfill bonded quilting batt.

Paper-backed fusible webbing for appliqué: 2 yards (183cm) 18" (46cm) wide (Pellon Wonder-Under).

Thread colors: White, golden brown, brown, cobalt blue, gray, dark gray, taupe, rust, ecru, gold. pink, peach, light gray-green, orange, silver metallic, gold metallic, variegated metallic and clear monofilament.

Tools and supplies: Sewing machine, scissors, iron, ruler, pins, copy paper (twelve to eighteen sheets), pencil, and mat board for template.

PROCEDURE

Make Paper Patterns for Each Teapot Full Size (for scaling up patterns see chapter 5)

Making the blocks

Note: Unless you were able to find all the listed fabric colors, you will probably have to lay out and work on all the blocks simultaneously to coordinate the colors.

1 Select fabric colors. Keep adjusting color choices until the overall harmonizes.

2 Cut out the background blocks, background fabrics, and teapots to size as given above.

3 Lay additional background fabrics on the background blocks and pin in place. Fold under raw edges within the block and top-stitch. Note that the horizontals of the appliqué pieces match on each row of blocks.

Technique for Machine-Appliqué of the Teapots
(see chapter 7 for more details)

1   Trace the teapot pattern on the back of the paper to get reversed patterns.

2   Place the paper-backed fusible webbing smooth side up over each pattern piece and trace. Cut out 1/4" (6mm) outside the outline.

3   Position the paper-backed fusible webbing pattern on the back of the teapot fabric, paying heed to fabric grain. Iron the webbing on using the cotton setting until it adheres.

Note: For the metallics, use HeatnBond, which adheres at a lower temperature.

4   Trim off the paper and fabric outside the pattern outline.

5   Position the teapot on the block. If it goes over a seam or other pronounced texture, stitch around the teapot shape and trim away the extra fabric. Iron the teapot on. Use a double layer of fabric for light fabrics that shadow through, bonding both layers if this occurs. Fuse on additional appliqué pieces for dimension or surface color change.

6   Since satin-stitching puckers or draws in most fabrics, stabilize the layers with a tearaway paper on the back.

7   Choose an appropriate color and satin-stitch embroider around the teapot and any added appliqué pieces. Don't leave any raw edges (Fig. 2-10).

8   Embellish the teapots as needed. Do this by machine embroidery using a variety of stitches: satin-stitch, pattern stitches, free-motion, or other; see chapter 6 on embroidery.

9   Tear off the backing paper or tearaway stabilizer.

2-10. A teapot block in process shows the flat brown teapot shape satin-stitch appliquéd to the background made from two Chinese embroidered tea towels and a soft green fabric.

Assemble the Quilt Face

1 Lay out the completed blocks and make any design changes needed.

2 Cut out the sashing, frame, and backing pieces. From the striped border fabric, cut four strips lengthwise, two 72" x 4" (183cm x 10cm) and two 56" x 4" (142cm) and two pieces 28" x 72" (71cm x 129cm) seamed together for backing (extra length allows for mitered corners).

For the eggshell-colored polycotton and/or eyelet sashings cut two 66" x 3-1/2" (167.5cm x 9cm) and two 51" x 3-1/2" (129.5cm x 9cm), two 57" x 2-3/4" (145cm x 7cm), two 51" x 2-3/4" (129.5cm x 7cm), and nine pieces 2-3/4" x 14-1/2" (7cm x 37cm). Cut both if the lace or eyelet needs backing.

3 Press the blocks. Use care with the metallic fabrics; flip over and press on the reverse side.

4 Align a 13-1/2" (34cm) template on the back of each finished block and trace a seam line with a pencil.

5 Align a 13-1/2" x 2-1/4" (34cm x 6cm) template to mark sashing seam lines; see chapter 1 on templates.

6 Assemble the blocks and sashing in this order:

a. Mark seam lines on the sashing back. Sew together four blocks and three sashings in three vertical rows.

b. Sew a sashing strip to each side of the center vertical row and mark the sashing seam lines to align with the other rows. Sew the first and third rows to the sashing, matching seams and marks.

c. Align, pin, and sew the top and bottom sashings in place. Repeat to join the side sashings.

d. To join the striped border pieces, leave 4-1/2" (11.5cm) of fabric at each corner for mitering. After joining the border pieces, align corners and sew a right-angle seam. Trim away the excess.

Note: At this point, some of the blocks lacked contrast with the sashing, so narrow ribbon edging was added for accent. On blocks where accent ribbon is noted, top-stitch it to border the block.

Assemble the Layers
(see chapter 9 for the envelope method)

1 Spread out bonded batting and spread the finished quilt top face up on the batting. Safety pin in both layers every 6" (15cm). Trim off extra batting.

2 Lay the seamed backing face down on the layers. Pin around the edges and machine-stitch. Begin 15" (38cm) from the bottom right corner and sew along the bottom edge toward the corner and up the side, stopping 4" (10cm) from the top. Sew across the top. Begin 4" (10cm) down from the top and sew the side and 15" (38cm) across the bottom. Lift up the backing and sew the quilt face to the batting across the opening (Fig. 2-11).

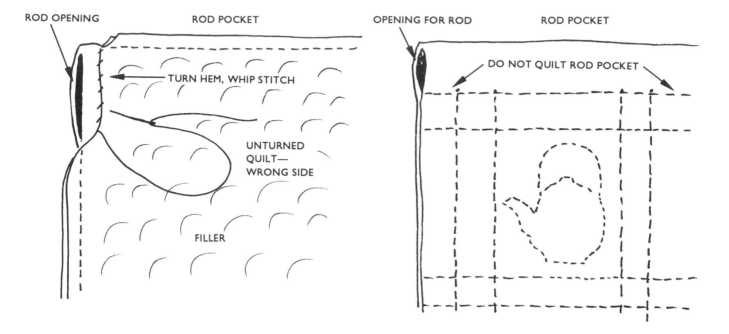

2-11. (Above) After sewing the layers together around the edges and turning to the right side, sew across the opening to join the quilt face to the bonded filler to keep it in place. Turn hems in the backing and the face/filler and blind-stitch closed.

2-12. (Above, right) To make a rod pocket, leave 4" (10cm) open at both sides of the top while stitching the edges together. Turn back a hem and hand-stitch before turning right side out. Don't quilt this area.

Technique for Making the Rod Pocket
(Fig. 2-12)

1 Trim away excess batting outside the seam line. Clip seam allowances across the bottom corners.

2 At the top, fold back the 4" (10cm) seam allowances left open and hand sew them to the batting in front and backing in back.

3 Turn the quilt envelope right side out. Press the edge seam flat from the reverse side of the quilt. Hand-stitch the bottom opening closed.

4 Lay the quilt flat and repin the safety pins to include the backing.

5 Stitch in the ditch along the sashing seam lines to quilt the surface; see the machine quilting section in chapter 9). Don't stitch the last 4" (10cm) on vertical quilting lines across the top. Leave this open for the rod pocket (Fig. 2-12).

6 Machine or hand quilt around the teapots.

PICTORIAL SPACE: MAKING A SCENE

Chapter Three

❖

"I want this scene to look real," you tell yourself, but how do you make this happen? A lot of help can come from artists' discoveries down through the ages, since they have coped with this same problem and come up with inventive solutions. This chapter reveals these methods in diagrams and shows examples of how modern art quilt makers use these same techniques. The Victorian Peabody House, made by the English-piecing technique in this chapter's project, is photographed in two views to show you how perspective works (Fig. 3-2, and see Figs. 3-8 and 3-9).

Once you have decided to make a quilted fabric picture, you face all the same delights and challenges any artist does in creating pictorial space. And you face the same pleasures and pitfalls of any quilter in creating a fabric construction. The success of these pieces is judged not only by technical sewing standards but by visual artistic standards.

This means that you need to create convincing images. You do not need to be an expert in drawing because there are many other ways to create imagery. Many of the fiber artists shown in this book used photographic images and applied them to fabric by various techniques, which will be covered in chapter 5. They also used other artists' design techniques which were covered in chapter 2, such as the process of arranging units and the idea of directing the viewer's eye.

Now for a quick tour though the ages. Don't be surprised if you find yourself saying, "I knew that!" as each era's discovery unfolds. All of this information is based on the way people see, so you probably do know these things instinctively. Now you can know them technically.

Representation: Making a Scene

Let's begin with point of view. Children make their scenes instinctively, often putting the ground in a stripe at the bottom, making the most important things the largest above this, and simplifying shapes to basics. That's the way the world looks to them. Six-year-old Hattie Stroud's quilt square from chapter 8 shows Martians settling down for a handcar ride (Fig. 3-1).

Realistic art is directly related to the way human eyes see the world. Without moving our heads, we can see clearly straight ahead, vaguely to the side, and not at all behind us. Our range of vision frames a scene. The location from which we

3-1. Six-year-old Hattie Stroud used linear/orthographic perspective without having any idea of what it is. She tipped up the railroad track the way she knows it looks with ties straight across, and put the handcar on it. The Martians float above. Oriental art often arranges pictorial space with this kind of logic.

33

3-2. The design was made from a photo of the Peabody House (now refurbished as lawyers' offices). This Victorian house wall quilt, 37" x 42" (94cm x 106.5cm), was made by English-style piecing (pattern and instructions are given in this chapter's instructions).

see the world is our point of view. (What kind of art would a lizard, who can swivel his eye all around, make?)

Children's drawings also express their opinions. Their drawings reveal what they like and what they think is important, beautiful, or intriguing. Taking a handcar ride with Martians would be fun. They also draw what is frightening, ugly, or mysterious. We all aim to do the same—establish a point of view and let the world know how we feel about it. We want the scenes we make to look and feel real so people will take seriously what we say, even if our message is lighthearted.

Illusion

Creating illusion for the artist does not mean to deceive but to counterfeit a three-dimensional reality on a flat surface. It is a necessary step in making paintings or picture quilts. Drawing lines to represent objects seems to be an instinctive skill among humans. Even as children, we select the essential lines to represent a real object. A round circle with two dots and a curved line in the right place is a face. We don't stop there. We try to draw better faces, more recognizable ones. The more accurate and detailed the representation, the greater the illusion of reality—as a rule.

Hearing a rule causes my mind to conjure up the many artworks that successfully flaunt that rule. Some artworks are the more effective for less detail, for being selective in simplifying the scene. Flaunting rules is a common challenge for an artist. In the quest to express the scene better, the artist strives to learn all the rules, techniques, and devices for creating artwork and then pushes beyond these limits. The artist has moved to the point where other rules apply.

How do you know which rule to follow or break, and in which direction to go? Each piece will dictate its own requirements. All the aspects of an artwork are interrelated and affect the choices for the others. Working with fabrics instead of paints affects your design. Drawing and painting tools produce lines, shapes, and colors so fluidly that they are easy to manipulate. With fabrics, texture will force itself to the fore, certain color choices may be complicated to achieve, and the shapes will be limited by technique.

Size, use, materials, and other choices will affect what you can accomplish in imagery. Some ways of working are detail-oriented, such as embroidery, and some are shape-oriented, such as appliqué. Some ideas are "heavy" and seem inconsistent with cozy techniques. To succeed best in making believable scenes be sensitive to the materials and techniques used and practice developing skill and judgment.

If all that sounds intimidating, it's enough to remember that each piece sets its own rules or expectations. These rules or devices have developed over time. A primitive scene can employ childlike representation in the drawing and be believable. An abstract scene can ignore photographic reality for expression through design. A realistic scene requires a more accurate perspective.

Representation of Objects

1. Flat Shapes: Scenes are made up of objects, so the first decision to be made is how to represent the object best. In her primitive style snow scene, Nancy Jane Collins makes each tree, cloud, horse or house a flat shape dependent on outline, color, and relationship to other objects for recognition (see C-7 in the color section). You know that roads and evergreens are not covered with calico flower patterns but you accept that working with cloth has certain characteristics and limitations. Each applied piece of fabric is cut out, hemmed, and hand sewn in place. This limits the details needed for reality, so you marvel that the flowers appear now to be snowflakes.

Primitive technique is a prime example of work dictating its own rules. The degree of simplification and stylization of objects is consistent throughout. Finding just the right calico print to represent texture and color is a major quest. The overall design of the scene is more important than the perspective. Primitives look deceptively easy to do, but you need a certain mind-set to be able to make one. Nancy Jane Collins is expert at this type of scene.

2. Shaded Shapes: Objects look more real if they are shaded rather than flat. Margaret Cusack in her portrait of George Washington reveals her secrets by mixing realities, part shaded and part something else (Fig 3-3). To begin, she based her imagery on a well-known American icon. She used machine-sewn appliqué on flat fabric pieces as Nancy Jane Collins does, but differently.

First, she analyzed the colors needed to represent highlights and shadows on the head. Unable to shade tones as in painting, Margaret accomplished this effect by laying tracing paper over the image and drawing lines where tones changed to divide one color from another. As many as eight or nine colors were needed to create a shaded effect, from the highlight on his brow to the darkest shadow on his neck. The satin-stitch thread lines used to appliqué the pieces exactly match the fabric pieces, effectively hiding the line. On his eyes and lips, where more detail was needed, contrasting thread color is used to outline features or add color, such as blue to the eye's iris.

3. Fooling with Reality: In other portraits she has done, Margaret Cusack uses this skillful device for creating shading for reality and stops there. In this one, she playfully overlays a patchwork grid pattern. With these disruptive squares she pushes our perception in two directions at once, back to Betsy Ross and patchwork quilts and forward to a television image breaking into pictels by computer-enhanced imagery. Here's another case of an artist pushing the rules aside for her own purposes.

4. Shading with Applied Color: Sometimes an easier way to shade objects done in fabrics is to use artist materials, such as paints, dyes, and pastels; see chapter 8 on color for details on doing this. Shading can be made with real dimension, as with quilting or trapunto, where the stuffed fabric takes on highlights and shadows. The first step in shading an object realistically is to study it carefully to discover where the shadows actually fall and what color they are. (You'll be surprised at your discoveries!)

Placing Objects in Space

Once an object becomes part of a scene, it should relate to the other objects in terms of reality. For example, a stick Martian would not fit in a primitive snow scene. The teapots on my quilt in chapter 2 (see Fig. 2-1) began more as pattern on a grid than objects sitting on a spatial plane. The more I made the background look like a tabletop, the more I had to cope with the laws of perspective. Perspective deals with how things look in space. The upper right teapot with the flat bottom as traced looks to be sitting on top of a table. When I moved the

3-3. Margaret Cusack used varied tones of fabric color to create three-dimensional shading on George Washington, 25" x 33" (63.5cm x 84cm). Photo: Millie Burns.

A.

B.

3-4. Looking at it straight-on, a teapot baseline is flat. Raise the horizon line and the baseline and lid curve to show the third dimension.

horizon line up, making the tabletop visible, I needed to curve the base of the pot so it appeared to be viewed slightly from above to look real (Fig. 3-4).

Creating Pictorial Space

All of the objects in a scene are subject to the same rules of perspective. Perspective means point of view, where you are standing to look at a scene. If the tabletop is shown, the teapot top must also be shown to carry out the illusion of reality. Perspective is the device by which the artist controls the viewer's eye. It is a way of drawing the viewer into the scene by establishing the viewer's viewing point.

Of course, artists break this rule, too, and fool with perspective for their own purposes, as Margaret Cusack did with shading, but we'll get to that later with some interesting examples.

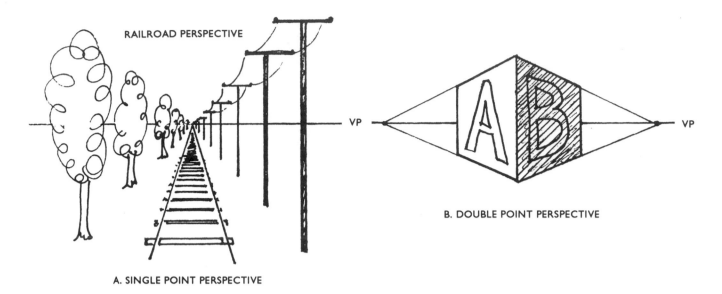

RAILROAD PERSPECTIVE

VP

VP

A. SINGLE POINT PERSPECTIVE

B. DOUBLE POINT PERSPECTIVE

3-5. Objects appear to diminish in size and disappear at a vanishing point, depending on your perspective.

Kinds of Perspective

The four most common types of perspective are:

1. Photographic   **2.** Linear   **3.** Aerial   **4.** Mixed

1. *Photographic Perspective:* The camera records a scene by capturing reflected light on the film in the form of highlights, shadows, and dark or light values. In the case of color film, it also captures color differences. Like the artist, the camera changes three-dimensional reality to a flat surface, making an illusion of reality.

The camera cannot provide opinion, move things around in the scene for better placement, or zero in on special details as a human can. It faithfully records the light and shadow coming in through the lens onto the film. It shows the scene as it sees it, unselectively. If some pictures are more effective than others, it is the artistic eye guiding the camera's eye that achieves this.

To make scenes as a camera sees them, you must use scientific perspective. In photographic reality, several things happen to the objects that show: they overlap each other, they are shaded by the light source, and they diminish in size as they disappear in the distance. Painters developed a scientific means of showing this by establishing vanishing points. In Fig. 3-5, the famous train track of grade school days appears to disappear in the distance by getting narrower and narrower, and the telephone poles grow shorter and shorter as they approach the vanishing point.

In this type of perspective, any and all the objects in a scene should obey the rules imposed by the vanishing points. Architects have large grid sheets marking off diminishing lengths as they recede in the distance. These charts allow for placing a building plan on the grid and accurately drawing the perspective without measuring it painstakingly (see Fig. 3-5).

2. *Linear Perspective:* A child, an engineer, or a Persian miniaturist would be apt to use linear perspective. In this, the train track remains the same width, as do other objects in the scene as they recede (Fig. 3-1). Hattie Stroud's train track stands up like a fence and the handcar appears transparent, drawn right over it in another color. She knows the ties on a train track run straight across and the handcar goes over it, so she drew them that way.

An engineer might need this kind of drawing to show three dimensions yet allow for accurate measurement of the parts (Fig. 3-6). Linear perspective gives a true picture showing actual dimensions. The technical geometric term for this is orthographic projection. An object is drawn actual size, or to scale, with projecting lines drawn perpendicular to the plane of projection. The value of this type of drawing is that any part can be measured to scale.

3. Aerial Perspective: Mapmakers use aerial perspective. This shows what you would see flying over a scene. It, like linear perspective, can have accurate dimensions for measuring distances. You might use this kind of perspective to make a quilt or a rug the viewer could look down on for a realistic point of view.

4. Mixed Perspective—Painters use any type of perspective—or even a mix of them—that they can make look right. Over the years, by observation and by experimentation, painters have developed ways of creating very realistic scenes. They represent space by graduations of color distinctness, by overlapping objects, by shifting the point of view, and by other means such as diminishing size. The following is a listing of the phases they went through to get there.

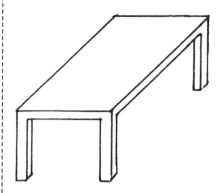

3-6. In linear perspective, the far side of the table measures the same as the front side. This is called orthographic projection.

Historic Development of Perspective

These are the kinds of perspective artists developed to create pictorial space:

1. Flat frontal   **3.** Foreshortened   **5.** Softened oblique
2. Complex frontal   **4.** Oblique

1. Flat Frontal: Early pictorial imagery was more concerned with recording an image on a cave wall or providing decoration on a Greek urn. It tended to use the most simple perspective of a straight-on frontal view. Yes, the ancient Egyptians used a curious combination of front and side views in the same figure, but you will notice that the handcar in Fig. 3-2 also shows top and side views at once. Artists do what they must to create their scenes. Most early art avoided perspective, using figures or objects in designs or close-up views with little distance shown.

In flat frontal perspective, the vertical and horizontal lines of a building or object are accurately shown all on one plane, with no angled side views (Fig. 3-7). Even though this is the oldest type of representation, it can still be used as shown in *Peabody House*, the project for this chapter (see Fig. 3-2).

For this piece, I photographed a charming old building in Birmingham, Michigan, now restored as an attorney's office, but formerly the Peabody House. My first shot showed a complicated angled view (Fig 3-8) not suitable for a pieced quilt design. I walked farther along the street to aim straight on. This eliminated most of the angled perspective and diminished the scene to one plane (Fig. 3-9). From this photo I was able to measure distances and make a scaled-up drawing as a pattern; see chapter 5 for details on this process to re-create your own building.

3-7. Ways to express perspective accurately in drawings, paintings, and tapestries developed over the centuries in this order: (1) flat-frontal; (2) complex-frontal; (3) foreshortened; and (4)

1.

2.

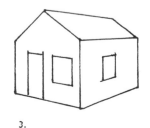

3.

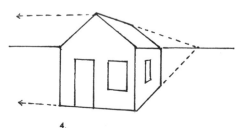

4.

3-8. This photo was taken to make a pattern for the Peabody House wall quilt. The perspective angle is softened oblique, a nice view, but not suitable for my purposes in this piece.

3-9. A few steps farther produced a photo that eliminated many angles, coming closest to early flat frontal perspective.

2. Complex frontal: The desire to show the side of a building brought about the next change. Artists pulled the side of the building around to the same plane as the front and showed them both in frontal views (see Fig. 3-7). As an example of these, see Margaret Cusack's *Nighttime* scene (see C-8 in the color section) and Nancy Jane Collins's farm scene (see C-7 in the color section). In both, the houses show both the front and side views on the same plane. This type of complex frontal perspective is typical of American primitives.

You'll notice that Margaret Cusack, who is basically a realist, instinctively uses diminishing perspective by angling the porch and tilting the roof. In addition, she uses a symmetrical balance with two houses up the center and one on each side. This is atypical of primitives, but the star-spangled sky fabric is most typical.

3. Foreshortened: The next step in the historic development of perspective was the discovery and use of the vanishing point, an arbitrary point where objects disappear in the distance. The flat views are replaced by foreshortened views (Fig. 3-7). If you drew lines following the edges of the buildings, the lines would converge at some point, this point being the vanishing point. Look at the walls in the room where you are sitting and notice that they appear to do the same. One wall might look flat frontal but the others will recede.

Of course, artists knew about vanishing points by observation, but at this point, a technical system of measuring was introduced, culminating in those architects' charts mentioned earlier.

4. Oblique: In this technique, both sides of the building or room are shown in perspective. Lines drawn along the contour of this architecture would show two vanishing points, one on each side (Fig. 3-7). Margaret Cusack's Christmas tree scene makes effective use of this technique (Fig. 3-10). She reverses the projection to show the inside of the room. The vanishing lines would cross at the center corner and converge in the distance on each side. Notice how all the furniture recedes to the vanishing points.

Margaret uses this type of perspective to focus attention on the Christmas tree. All lines converge there, drawing your eyes directly on it. Nice to have such a device at hand, isn't it?

5. Softened Oblique: Oblique perspective, standing right at the center of the scene, can be harsh. Most artists use a softened oblique showing more of one side than the other (see Fig. 3-7) My photo of the Peabody House (see Fig. 3-8) is a prime example of softened oblique. This is the most common perspective artists use in scenes, probably because it focuses on one side more than another.

3-10. *In O Christmas Tree, a fabric collage featured on a plate edition, Margaret Cusack used shallow depth and two-point perspective in order to use print fabrics with no perspective angle. Photo: Ron Breland.*

Organizing Space in a Scene

1. Changing the view: Now that you know all these types of perspective you can play games with the viewer and plot how the viewer will see your scene. You can control the viewer's eyes. In some large paintings artists alter the perspective of parts of the picture to make the scene look as if the viewer is turning his head to see each part of it. Each object appears in the perspective related to the angle from which the viewer sees it. You can make the viewer look up or down. In my *Self Portrait* (See Fig. 8-8 in chapter 8) I drew exactly what I saw when I looked down. Friends puzzle, then they laugh to realize that they are looking through my eyes, seeing what I saw.

Most scenes are more subtle than this, and you are not aware of being controlled by the artist as to where to look. The primary requirement in working with unusual perspectives is to keep the vertical true. You can get away with divergent recession, multiple vanishing points, and other tricks if you have true verticals and horizontals in logical orderliness.

2. *Bird's-Eye View:* A characteristic of the primitives is the common use of a bird's-eye-view perspective. A camera view of the countryside would overlap objects distractingly. Moving the viewer's vantage point up allows for making each object separate, with less overlap. The perspective is no longer scientifically true, but it looks just as logical to the viewer.

Marilyn Price uses a bird's-eye view in her scene of fields (see C-9 in the color section). Knowing that you could not see all this from the road, she changed a horizontal scene to a vertical one by tipping up the scene. You are lifted to view through a bird's eye. Then she puts a decorative border of flat frontal flowers around three sides to frame it. This is what you might see if you entered the scene and stopped to pick a flower. Yet this use of dual perspective irritated one person on seeing this piece, who said, "That's not the way it is."

3. *Lower Point of View:* Sue Pierce takes you on a different tour in her piece *Poolesville Town Hall* (see C-10 in the color section). She walks you up to a building and says, "Look up." In this scene she maintains scientific perspective, as a camera would see it. Follow the building's lines and you discover that the perspective angles from the bottom to a vanishing point above the center top. Artists commonly use a lower viewpoint to make the viewer feel smaller and to generate awe.

4. *Shallow Ground Perspective:* One easy form of perspective to use is shallow ground. Everything sits in the foreground, perhaps against a close-in wall. There's no middle ground, so nothing need recede in the distance. The objects are featured in this scene, much like a theater stage. Margaret Cusack does this in Fig. 8-5 in chapter 8.

The purpose of your scene suggests the type of perspective you might use. Don't be concerned that this will be complicated to decide. Most of these decisions are instinctive. A few of the artists whose pieces I've been analyzing as to perspective may be just as surprised as you to see what they've done.

5. *Size:* In their drawings, children ignore the rules of diminishing size of objects as they recede in the distance. Almost nothing recedes; all objects appear on one plane. Size in their work relates to importance. Young children often draw themselves the largest, followed by Mom, Dad, or the dog, depending on the child's point of view. Some religious paintings do the same thing. In a historic hospital in Europe, I saw an early wall mural that showed the deity as the largest figure in the center, with the donors to the hospital who paid for the mural next in size to the side and the common folk smallest across the bottom. This perspective was based on importance not science.

Other Cultures

Ancient Chinese and Islamic paintings aimed for a far different goal than photo-realism. Decorative surface has been paramount for them above imitative naturalism. They avoid box interiors, which force perspective. They tilt tabletops for an orthographic bird's-eye view, as I did on the teapot quilt (see Fig. 2-1 in chapter 2). They make their scenes vertical and stack up the elements of the scene as you might come across them in increasing distance. Lee Porter does this in Fig. 1-6 and so do the American primitives of Nancy Jane Collins in chapter 1 (see Fig. 1-7).

Types of perspective vary within these scenes controlled by the qualities of the object, its size, and its relationship to the whole scene. In order to tell what small objects are, they are pictured obliquely, at an angle. Large ones are shown frontally, with the emphasis on decorative pattern. These artworks are just as satisfying in their way as the scientifically correct pieces are in theirs.

Different cultures have preferences for various types of perspective and pictorial arrangement. All of us are influenced by our native culture, including everything from traditional artworks to what we see on television, in magazines, and on billboards. In reality, you have the perspective devices of the whole world to use in your artworks. Use any kind you wish. Your goal is to keep on reworking your preliminary sketches (or however you work) until the scene does what you want.

In the project below, the technique of piecing required a geometric-style pattern, and flat frontal perspective best provided this. In turn, English-style piecing gives the accuracy that an architectural scene requires. The technique and the imagery have chosen each other.

3-11. The center panel pattern for the
Peabody House quilt, plus partial border
design (see Fig. 3-1 for entire pattern).
Scale it up to size.

PROJECT: PERSPECTIVE, *PEABODY HOUSE*
(Fig. 3-2 and 3-11; see C-11 in the color section)

Overview: This quilted wall hanging shows how to make a house by pieced patchwork. Both English and American piecing techniques are used, with tiny details appliquéd on. Instructions for making a geometric pattern of your house from a photograph are mentioned below and are described fully in chapter 5.

Theme: Technically, my goal was to use the archaic style of flat frontal perspective combined with photo-realism to show the similarities. As for imagery, this is one of the few buildings in our town that has maintained its character over the years. I've always enjoyed seeing it, so I decided to do its portrait. You can choose between English-style piecing or American hand- or machine-piecing.

Techniques: (1) English-style, hand-sewn pieced patchwork provides great accuracy for a complex pattern; (2) American hand- and machine-sewn patchwork; (3) hand and machine appliqué; and (4) adding edging.

Size: Overall 37" x 42" (94cm x 106.5cm); central design unit 22-1/2" x 27" (57cm x 68.5cm).

MATERIALS

Note: For best results in hand-sewing, use lightweight, firmly woven cotton or polycotton fabric from the quilting section in your fabric store.

House scene: 1/4 yard (23cm) of these colors: deep rust red, brick red, pin-dot brick red, warm white, striped (white, blue, tan, and rust), gray, gray print (circles), gray print (dots), dark gray textured, black, brown, and green paisley. For the tan, use framing below.

Background: 2/3 yard (61cm) navy blue with tan dots; border: twenty-six blocks of four triangles (104 triangles) 3" x 5" (7.5cm x 12.5cm) including seam allowance; finished size block: 4-1/2" (11.5cm) square.

Frame and backing: 1-2/3 yards (152cm) tan 45" wide (112.5cm).

Edging: 12" (30.5cm) maroon with flower print 45" (114cm) wide.

Window sashes: 2 yards (183cm) 3/16" wide (4.5mm) ribbons in maroon, black, and off-white.

Filler: 38" x 42" (96.5cm x 106.5cm) bonded batting fiberfill; threads to match, paper-backed fusible web (for example, Wonder-Under).

Tools and supplies: Sewing machine (optional), Teflon sheet (or parchment paper), needles, scissors, iron, ruler, paper, T square or triangle, and freezer paper (optional).

PROCEDURE

Technique for English Hand-Pieced Patchwork
(Fig. 3-12)

1 If you plan to do your own house instead of the project given, photograph your house as close to front-on as you can (flat frontal perspective) and scale up by measuring as shown in chapter 5. Use as many straight lines as possible for joining seams and plan to assemble it in units.

2 On paper, make two full-sized plans of the center panel. The first, called the "plan," serves as a guide in checking progress as you quilt. Use the second, called the "template pattern," to cut up as template patterns. Trace each window on a separate paper for appliqué patterns. Use a pencil and a T square or triangle to be sure of straight lines; see chapter 4 for using drafting tools.

3 On the plan, number the pattern pieces and note fabric color.

4 Turn the template pattern over and, on the reverse side, number each piece the same as on the plan. Mark an arrow to indicate up and the grain line on each piece.

5 Cut the template pattern apart exactly on the lines except for two instances:

  a. Cut the right-hand roof piece with no notch in the lower left corner. Cut the roof eaves as shown in the photo and allow the corner to overlap.

  b. Don't trim out the windows. Appliqué the windows and cornices on later. (You can piece the windows if you wish but the cornices would be close to impossible to manage.)

6 Arrange the templates on the back side of appropriate fabrics, paying attention to grain line and print design, and be sure to leave 1/4" (6.5mm) or more seam allowance all around each piece. Pin in place and cut out the fabric pieces, keeping them pinned together.

7 Carefully fold the seam allowances over the paper template and finger-press them in place. To keep the seam allowance in place, you have several choices: baste it through the paper template, use freezer paper wax side up and iron the edges, tape or glue-stick the edges down, or press it and keep the pins in place.

8 To join abutting pieces, align the folded edges, right sides facing. Whip-stitch along the edge with tiny stitches to overcast the seam avoiding sewing into the paper as much as possible. Pull the stitches firmly to make a tight seam but not so firmly as to pucker the seam. This seam will open out flat (Fig. 3-12). (It is possible to machine sew this seam if you are incredibly accurate, but then you might as well use the American technique which follows on page 48.)

3-12. In English-style piecing, fabric pieces are made by folding hems over paper templates. Folded edges are aligned, fabric pieces face-to-face, and tightly whip-stitched together.

ENGLISH PIECING

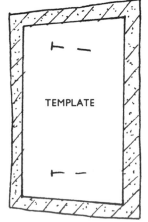
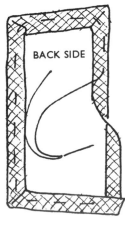
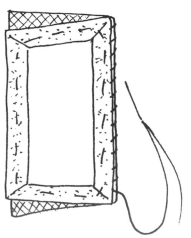
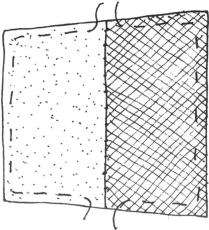

A. FOLD FABRIC OVER PAPER TEMPLATE
AND STITCH, TAPE, OR PRESS TO ADHERE.

B. ALIGN THE EDGES
AND WHIP-STITCH.

C. RIGHT SIDE.
(REMOVE BASTING WHEN
PIECE IS COMPLETED.)

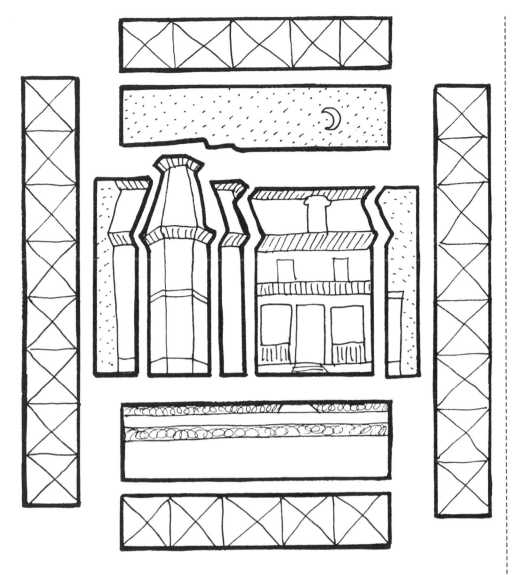

3-13. *Assemble the quilt pieces in units, joining each assembled section to the next larger section, as shown by the diagram.*

9 Use the plan to assemble the house. Assemble the pieces within an area into a larger unit, and then join these units. Use this order or devise your own (Fig. 3-13):

a. First, assemble the tower roof, then the tower itself, and join into a vertical unit at the eaves.

b. Next, assemble the right-hand roof unit, the upper windows unit, and the porch section. Join these into a vertical unit.

c. Join the left-hand roof, eaves, and house.

d. Join these vertical sections to complete the house. Join the edge sky and building pieces to complete the center of the panel.

e. Join the grass, sidewalk, and road into a horizontal unit, and join to the house. Join the sky to the house at the top.

10 Remove the basting stitches, tape, or pins. The paper templates can remain in place. They will act as a stabilizer for appliquéing the windows on.

AMERICAN PIECING

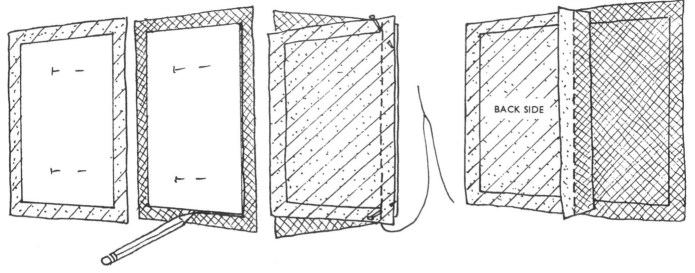

A. TRACE AROUND TEMPLATE.   B. PIN THROUGH DRAWN SEAM LINE
AND STITCH BY HAND OR MACHINE.

3-14. In American piecing, seam lines are drawn on the piece backs. Pieces are aligned face-to-face, seams pinned, and lines seamed by hand or machine.

Technique for American Hand or Machine Piecing (Fig. 3-14)

Note: You can mix the methods, as I did, using hand and machine sewing. Just don't let any traditional quilters catch you doing it.

Follow steps 1 to 6 from above and continue with the following step 7:

7 Using a pencil, trace a seam line carefully around the templates. Add 1/4" (6mm) or more seam allowance and cut out the pieces.

8 To join, align pieces right sides facing. Stick pins through the drawn seam lines top, piece corner to under piece corner, and secure the pins across the line. If the seam is long, align and place pins along the seam line.

9 Hand or machine sew exactly on the drawn seam line. Press the seam allowances to one side or open the seam allowances to each side.

10 Assemble the pieces as above.

Finishing the *Peabody House* Scene

1 Use the window and cornice patterns to cut out the pattern pieces of their appropriate fabric colors. If you are hand appliquéing, turn under a 1/4" (6mm) seam allowance all around and press a hem. For machine appliqué, leave no seam allowance. Use fusible webbing if you wish.

2 Cut and hem the cornices first and hand- or machine-stitch in place or use nonfray ribbon and machine appliqué in place.

3 Align and straight-stitch the curtains and windows in place. Use fusible webbing, if you wish.

4 Cut the ribbon window woodwork long enough for a short tuck under at the ends. For hand sewing, pin or cello-tape the ribbons in place overlapping the curtain and/or window edges and sew. For machine sewing, iron fusible webbing on the back of the ribbons and iron them over the window edges. If you use fusible webbing, use a Teflon cloth or parchment paper underneath to prevent sticking.

Note: With such narrow ribbon, it is difficult to iron on the fusible webbing and easy to iron sticky webbing residue on the quilt face. Try this. Cut 5" (12.5cm) pieces of ribbon and lay them side by side on freezer paper and iron to adhere. Cut paper-backed fusible webbing to size and iron on. Pull off the freezer paper. Cut the fusible-backed ribbons apart and peel to use.

5 Appliqué the moon in place using fusible webbing.

Assemble the Border

1 Use the English or American style to piece the border squares. Sew them into two strips of six and two strips of seven squares.

2 Mark the seam lines and sew the six square strips to the sides of the central house panel. Sew the remaining strips to the top and bottom.

3 If you want a larger quilt or wall hanging, sew additional strips of framing to the house block to complete the quilt face. I used a light border. See the diagram for dimensions.

Assembling Layers
(see chapter 9 for the traditional method of finishing a quilt)

1 Spread out the backing face down, add the bonded batting on top of the backing, and lay the completed quilt face on top.

2 Align the edges, trim away extra backing or batting, and secure the layers with safety pins at 4" to 6" (10cm to 15cm) intervals, avoiding seam lines.

3 Use a hoop or frame to hand-quilt in the ditch or 1/8" (3mm) inside the edge or machine-quilt in the ditch.

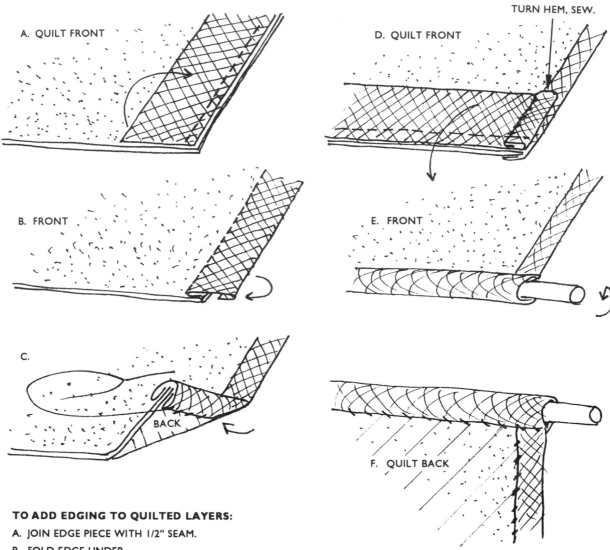

A. QUILT FRONT

B. FRONT

C.

BACK

D. QUILT FRONT

TURN HEM, SEW.

E. FRONT

F. QUILT BACK

TO ADD EDGING TO QUILTED LAYERS:

A. JOIN EDGE PIECE WITH 1/2" SEAM.

B. FOLD EDGE UNDER.

C. WRAP EDGING OVER QUILT EDGE AND HAND OR MACHINE STITCH.

D. FIRST, TURN HEM AT END AND SEW. THEN JOIN EDGING TO QUILT
   AS ABOVE (A.) WITH 1/2" SEAMS.

E. FOLD EDGE UNDER (B), WRAP EDGE OVER QUILT EDGE
   (LEAVE ROOM FOR ROD).

F. INSERT ROD, HAND STITCH EDGING ON BACK SIDE.

3-15. To add edging to quilted layers, join side edging pieces with a 1/2" (1.5cm) seam, wrap over the edge, turn under 1/2" (1.5cm), and whip-stitch to the backing. Hem the ends of the top and bottom edging first. Leave the top ends open for a rod.

4 When the piece is fully quilted, measure and cut the edges straight. Sew 2-1/2" (6cm) wide edge binding around the quilt face in this manner: Cut the side edging to fit in length, lay the edging and quilt face to face, aligning the edges, and seam 1/2" (1.5cm) in from the edge (Fig. 3-15). Wrap the edging over the quilt edge, turn under 1/2" (1.5cm), and hand-stitch to the quilt back. Repeat for the top and bottom, except for this: First, cut the edging 2" (5cm) longer and make a hem at each end. Join the edging as above. Leave the top ends open to insert a narrow hanging rod.

THE WORKSHOP: USING ARTIST TOOLS

Chapter Four

❖

A workshop can be as small as a sewing basket full of threads, needles, scissors, pins, measures, and markers (Fig. 4-1). This will soon build to a larger collection to make your projects easier, quicker, and more accurate. Good-quality tools and supplies, along with storage and a space in which to work, are vitally important to creativity. Quilters with predetermined patterns can work in small spaces, but a pictorial quilter will need more space to lay out and view work as the piece progresses.

This chapter talks about sewing tools and new products, art materials, office supplies, and drafting equipment that quilters often use. Techniques will describe how to make a working or display wall, how to make a light box, and how to use drafting tools to make patterns, such as the *Game Quilt* project (see Fig. 4-2).

To do good projects, you must feel that your creations are important enough to use good materials and quality tools. Nothing is more frustrating than thread that twists or breaks, needles with holes too small to thread, scissors that saw rather than slice through fabric, rusty pins, or a floppy tape measure. Poor or wrong tools will quickly ruin your enjoyment for doing projects. Once you acquire these good tools, treasure them and preserve them from your household; you can always provide alternative tools for others in your family.

My studio has miscellany tucked in everywhere. The best thing about the room is that I can leave my projects out while they are in progress. I love this room, but there was a time when I worked on the dining room table and stored stuff under the bed. If you cannot carve out an entire workshop for yourself, try for a basic tool collection, portable equipment, and inventive storage, all to be discussed later in this chapter.

I have decided that my studio is not a chaotic mess, despite appearances, but a cluster of overlapping workstations. These stations include centers for drawing, designing (using the floor or a wall), construction, sewing, and writing. They share space, serve double duty, and can be "put away" when necessary. Here's how this works.

4-1. A sewing basket of basics may be all you need, or may be only the beginning of your collection of tools and supplies.

4-2. The Game Quilt *pictures traditional games—all more than sixty years old— done in geometric precision. Tools for drawing accurately are listed in this chapter and a pattern for the quilt given at the end of this chapter.*

THE DRAWING CENTER

This area includes a drawing board, a magnifying lamp, a light box, storage drawers for paper and tools, a paper cutter for both paper and fabric cutting, and drafting tools.

If you say you can't draw a straight line, take heart—nobody can without using a guide. Yet straight lines or true circles are needed in quilt making. For example, the grid pattern is easier to measure and draw than to trace. Tracing often must be neatened and made accurate on the drafting board. Using the following drafting tools and techniques will help you make "true" patterns.

Techniques for Drawing Accurate Lines

Your workshop supplies should include a drawing board with sliding ruler or a drawing pad, a T square, a forty-five-degree triangle, a protractor, a compass, sharp No. 2 (or harder) pencils, an eraser, a 24" (60cm) ruler, a 1" (2.5cm) wide strip of cardboard, and six or more sheets of paper at least 20" (51cm) square or a roll of paper 20" (51cm) wide (Fig. 4-3).

1. Squares: Here are three ways to make an accurate square:

 1. Tape paper to your drawing board under the ruler. Draw a measured baseline along the sliding ruler edge. Align a right-angle (forty-five degree) triangle with each end of the baseline and draw verticals along the triangle edge. Move the sliding ruler up the measured distance and draw the closing line (Fig. 4-4).

 2. To draw a square with the T square, affix your paper to a work surface, drawing pad, or table. Align the T square along the side and draw a measured baseline in from the edge. Measure up and draw a parallel line. Use a triangle, as above, or move the T square to the bottom edge, align it with the mark, and draw vertical lines.

 3. If you have no drafting equipment except a tape measure and this book, trace the right edge and bottom to make a right angle. Measure the right edge and align the book corner up the edge and across the top. Measure the top, align the book, and draw the left side. Fold the paper into a triangle to check for accuracy.

2. Grids: To make a grid, begin with a sheet of paper large enough. Draw a baseline across the bottom and mark off even intervals the size you want. At the first mark, draw a vertical line and mark this line off at the same intervals. Align the T square or slide the triangle along the ruler, stopping at each baseline mark to draw vertical lines. Slide the ruler up or shift the T square to stop at each mark and draw across.

3. Angled Lines: To draw angled lines, as on a backgammon board, make an 18" (46cm) square. Draw a measured baseline and mark off even intervals of 1-1/2" (4cm). Measure up the length of the angled lines and draw a horizontal line at 7-3/4" (20cm). On this line, measure in half the width of the long triangle—3/4" (2cm)—and mark. From this point, mark the same even intervals across the line—1-1/2" (4cm)—ending with a half interval 3/4" (2cm). Draw a line from the bottom corner to the half interval mark on the line. Repeat across making lines from the base marks to the top interval marks (Fig. 4-5).

4. Circles: To make large circles use a compass or cut a strip of cardboard 2" (5cm) longer than half the width of the circle (the radius). Punch a tack 1"

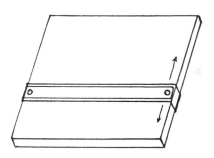

4-3. *Common drafting tools include: a drawing board with a straight-edge sliding rule for geometric drawing;*

a T square for straight lines perpendicular to an edge;

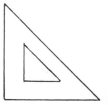

a forty-five-degree triangle for right-angle corners;

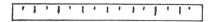

a ruler for measuring;

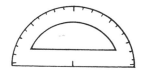

a protractor for measuring angles;

and a compass for drawing circles.

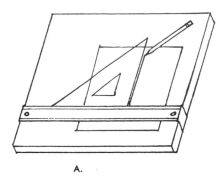

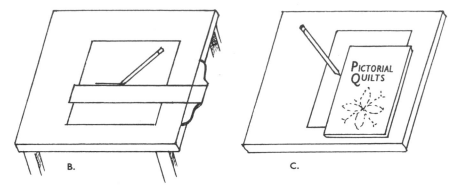

A.

B.

C.

4-4. (a) *To make accurate drawings, tape paper on the drawing board, draw horizontal lines with the sliding rule and vertical lines with the triangle on the rule;* **(b)** *align the T square with the table edge to draw horizontal and vertical lines; and* **(c)** *use this book as a right angle; rotate it for the next side of a square.*

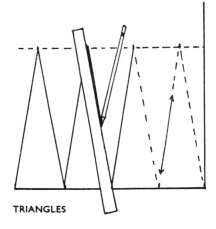

TRIANGLES

4-5. *To make the backgammon board triangles, measure even intervals across the baseline, measure even intervals across a mid-line that are off-set from the baseline intervals, and connect the dots.*

(2.5cm) from one end into the center of your paper or push the tack up through the paper and strip, and then cap with a cork or eraser. For a 6" (15cm) circle, measure 3" (7.5cm) from the tack and punch a hole for the pencil tip. Hold the pencil vertical and draw by circling around the tack (Fig. 4-6).

For a small circle use a circle guide to trace them.

5. Sectioned Circles: To divide circles into parts you need a protractor marked with the degrees of angle.

1. Draw a line across the circle, passing exactly through the center (the tack hole). Place the protractor on this line with its center in the center of the circle. Align the ruler from the center through the degree mark desired and draw a line to the edge of the circle. Repeat for each line, keeping the protractor in place for each half of the circle.

2. If you don't have a protractor, use the diagram on page 55. The lines you need are marked: eighteen degrees for the dart board and sixty degrees for the Chinese checkers. Align the corner of the angle A on the center tack. Mark along the angle B line to the circle edge, rotate to align the angled line C with the drawn line, and mark line B again. Repeat all around the circle.

To make the dart board pattern use the eighteen-degree angle to make twenty even spaces. Use the cardboard circle drawing strip, measure along it from the center and punch holes at 1/2" (1.5cm), 3-1/2" (8.5cm), 4" (10cm), 6" (15cm), and 6-1/2" (16.5cm). Draw circles at these points; see Fig. 4-7 and the quilt pattern.

To make the Chinese checkers board's six-pointed star divisions, use the sixty-degree angle. Mark these divisions at the edge of the circle. For the star, draw a line from one mark to the second mark over. Continue doing this around the circle to make overlapping triangles or use the pattern for a star segment with dot pattern provided, and trace twelve meshed triangles in a star shape (Fig. 4-8).

6. Line Guides: To neaten randomly made or traced pattern lines, use a French curve or a flexible guide. Match the guide to part of the line and draw. Continue drawing sections until the complete line is drawn.

Useful Papers

1. Packages of five hundred sheets of the cheapest white copy paper are fine for sketching, making patterns, stabilizing fabrics for machine stitching, keeping notes, cleaning the iron, transferring drawings, and for the grandchildren to draw on.

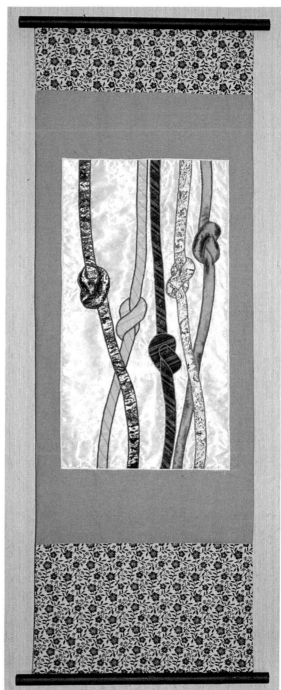

C-1. *(left) Erma Martin Yost used a variety of techniques to create Spirit Pass, 32" x 38" (81cm x 97cm). She dye-printed, machine-embroidered, and re-assembled quilt pieces in rich Southwest colors. Photo: Noho Gallery, NYC.*

C-3. *Marilyn Price's GTE Commission, 4' x 5' (122cm x 152cm), made for GTE in Fort Wayne, Indiana, was done in block that forms a non-traditional design in this photo-silkscreen and quilted-cotton wall quilt.*

C-2. *Knot Kakimono shows a simple knot used as a design motif in a project you can make from directions given in chapter 1, which also tells how and where to get good ideas for quilting projects.*

C-4. *Marilyn Price designed this cheerful wall quilt, 3' x 8' (94cm x 244cm), for St. Catherine's Hospital in East Chicago, Indiana. She combined the frame made of quilt squares with an intermeshing "brick half-drop" block pattern in her design.*

C-5. *Joyce Carey says, "...I discovered dozens of Chinese Jacquard-woven portraits, just as the Communist regime was beginning to crumble. I'm having fun making them into political cartoons." She combines three different basic units in her network: the woven or quilted imagery squares, a parallelogram strip, and a smaller red square, size: 45" square (113cm). Photo: Artist.*

C-6. *For Family Teapots, an informal collection of teapots served as an idea for imagery to be appliquéd on a traditional grid quilt design. See chapter 2 for ways to design and arrange your ideas into a quilt.*

C-7. Nancy Jane Collins, an expert primitive quilter, used cotton fabrics cut in uncomplicated shapes, hemmed, and hand-appliquéd. Your eyes make the printed flower fabric into stones in the road. Called Sleigh Ride, her quilting is displayed in a frame, painting style. Photo: Burge Photography; Owners: Dr. and Mrs. Edwin Barrow.

C-9. Marilyn Price uses perspective to move your eye up for a birds-eye view in Peninsula Patchwork, 26" x 34" (60.5cm x 86.5cm), and then move you close enough to touch the flowers in the frame. For centuries artists have known how to portray and mix perspectives in paintings.

C-8. In her collage illustration, Nighttime, 20" x 14" (51cm x 35.5cm), Margaret Cusack aimed for a primitive style by using complex frontal perspective in the center top house and mixed perspective in the others. Photo: Skip Caplan; Owner: Kwikset Locks.

C-10. In Poolesville Town Hall, 40" x 48" (101.5cm x 122cm), Sue Pierce places you down low in front of the building, looking up. Perspective means point of view.

C-11. In Peabody House, the author took a photograph in flat frontal perspective to create a quilt pattern for English-style pieced quilting. To make this or your own house, see chapter 3.

C-12. Game Quilt was made geometrically accurate by using artist's drafting tools. For the pattern and information on making this, see chapter 4.

C-13. Rosemary Reid made a 40th anniversary quilt for her parents by printing 194 collected photographs on light sensitive muslin squares, piecing them together in a traditional quilt pattern.

C-14. Marilyn Pierce in Summer Promise, 5' x 4' (152cm x 122cm), screen printed images with toned colors on fabrics, heat set the colors, and then quilted around the shapes for added dimension.

C-15. In Amigos, Marilyn Price used a combination of photographic imagery, hand-drawn leaves and birds, and dyed color strips, and then quilted with patterned machine stitching.

C-17. For Little Red Riding Hood, a family photo was used to make a fabric appliquéd portrait; directions for doing this appear in chapter 5.

C-16. Margaret Cusack appliquéd a picture projected on fabric, Vacirea Portrait, 20" x 31" (51cm x 79cm), skillfully limiting choices to a few colors and adding a harmonizing border print fabric. Photo: Skip Caplan; Owner: Ida Vacirea.

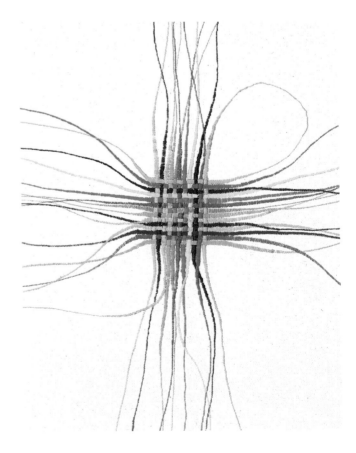

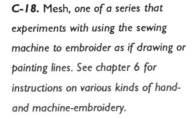

C-18. Mesh, one of a series that experiments with using the sewing machine to embroider as if drawing or painting lines. See chapter 6 for instructions on various kinds of hand- and machine-embroidery.

C-19. The Hall Family Quilt, 46" x 50" (117cm x 127cm) was hand embroidered by Hall children in about 1925, from printed transfer designs, then commercially available. You can make your own transfer designs now, with transfer pencils available from craft stores.

C-20. Did you ever wonder how it feels to take a bungee cord leap? B. J. Adams knows and shows us in Bungy Attitude (proper Australian spelling) 19" x 26" (48cm x 66cm). This satin-stitch machine embroidery shows her view from space. Photo: Bill Pellitier.

C-22. *Again Margaret Cusack dips into her storage for just the right fabrics. She used assorted colors and a variety of weaves in her fabrics to appliqué for collage illustration, SSMC Streetscene, 16" x 21" (40cm x 53cm). Photo: Ron Breland.*

C-21. *(opposite) Mary Gentry's Quilt, 41" x 82" (102.5cm x 205cm) sneaks up on you. Its color, fabric textures, and crazy-quilt style design are so appealing, all done in hand-embroidery stitching. Yet the imagery shows all the perils of contemporary life.*

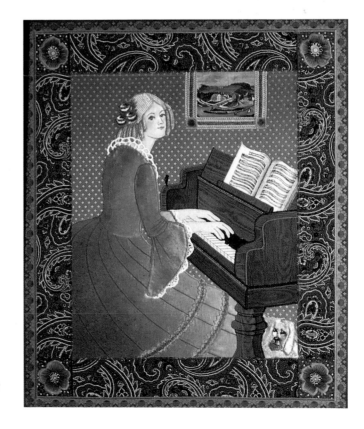

C-23. *Margaret Cusack took advantage of printed fabrics to create wallpaper, wood graining, and even a framed scene in her appliqué, Young Woman at the Piano, 19" x 23" (48cm x 58cm). Photo: Ron Breland.*

C-24. *Fusible webbing was used to hold appliqué pieces in place for machine embroidering on Carousel Horse Tote Bag. To make this or other kinds of hand or machine appliqué, see chapter 7.*

C-25. *Janet Page-Kessler's exotic flowers bloom in equally exotic colors in After the Fall, 31" x 42" (79cm x 107cm). Using imaginative colors is one of the major delights of making fiber art.*

C-26. *What commercially printed fabrics lacked, Margaret Cusack made up for by using various dyes and paints to achieve the effect she wanted in April Showers, 15" x 16" (38cm x 41cm). Even the flowers shade from cloudy blue to sunny pink and yellow.*

C-27. *B. J. Adams in Mixed Metaphor 28" x 42" (42cm x 107cm), used familiar stitcher's tools as imagery to appliqué this cheerful wall quilt. Photo: Berger and Associates, Kensington, Maryland.*

C-29. To get the shaded tones of sky Margaret Cusack dipped the background fabric in blue Rit dye on this Thailand Airlines advertisement.

C-28. (opposite) Mary Gentry's wall quilt Chicago Community Gardens , 54" x 76" (137cm x 193cm), is painted with Procion dyes, then hand- and machine-quilted. Photo: Bill Pellitier.

C-30. Hattie's Quilt is a crayon transfer quilt with blocks drawn by 6 year old Hattie Stroud. To try this delightful project for kids and grownups alike, see chapter 8.

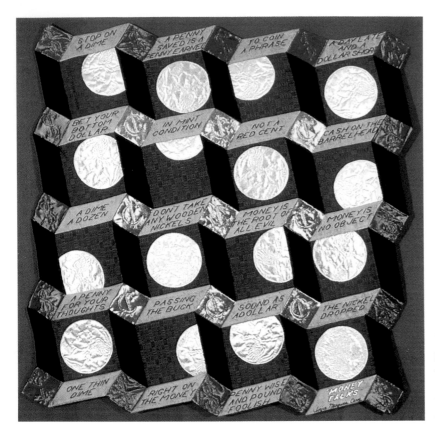

The quilt shows the following phrases:

STOP ON A DIME · A PENNY SAVED IS A PENNY EARNED · TO COIN A PHRASE · A DAY LATE AND A DOLLAR SHORT · BET YOUR BOTTOM DOLLAR · IN MINT CONDITION · NOT A RED CENT · CASH ON THE BARRELHEAD · A DIME A DOZEN · DON'T TAKE ANY WOODEN NICKELS · MONEY IS THE ROOT OF ALL EVIL · MONEY IS NO OBJECT · A PENNY FOR YOUR THOUGHTS · PASSING THE BUCK · SOUND AS A DOLLAR · THE NICKEL DROPPED · ONE THIN DIME · RIGHT ON THE MONEY · PENNY WISE AND POUND FOOLISH · MONEY TALKS

C-31. *Joyce Marquess Carey used metallic fabrics of silver and copper in* Money Talks, *43" x 43" (109cm x 109cm), to show pennies and dimes for this wall quilt designed for a bank. Photo: Artist.*

C-32. *The reverse side of Mary Gentry's* Chicago Community Gardens, *54" x 76" (137cm x 193cm), shows how she builds dimensional shape with machine-quilting and hand-stitching.*

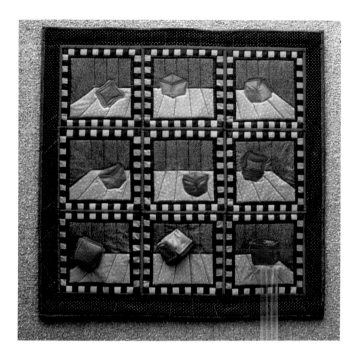

C-33. *In* Escape from Block Nine, *48" x 48" (122cm x 122cm), Sue Pierce's blocks progress from flat quilting through increased dimension until one gains full dimension and sits on its own pedestal.*

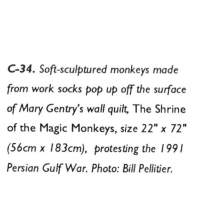

C-34. *Soft-sculptured monkeys made from work socks pop up off the surface of Mary Gentry's wall quilt,* The Shrine of the Magic Monkeys, *size 22" x 72" (56cm x 183cm), protesting the 1991 Persian Gulf War. Photo: Bill Pellitier.*

C-35. Favorite Cats shows Hall family cats used as models for the fur-textured fabric appliques. They are embellished with machine embroidery and "glass" toy-animal eyes to simulate real cats. To make a quilt from a range of fabrics, see the directions in chapter 9.

2. For sketching, tracing, and overlay drawing, use tracing paper. It comes in various sizes of pads or rolls.

3. Newsprint or a roll of wrapping paper is good for large plans or patterns.

4. Freezer paper is handy for adhering paper to fabric by ironing.

5. Grocery store parchment paper works to resist fusible webbing.

Handy Tapes

Five handy tapes—in addition to sewing tapes—include duct tape, transparent tape, natural and colored masking tape, and packaging tape.

Markers

A range of markers is needed since no one marker is going to do it all. Use an ordinary No. 2 graphite pencil for drawing template seam lines on the back side of fabrics, to trace cutting lines on the front side of fabrics, or to make lines to be satin-stitched over. Use pressed chalk disks, chalk pencils, or marking wheels to lay a line that will easily brush off or sew marking "tacks" and remove stitches later.

Be sure you know what kind of marker you are using. Inks may migrate to the surface later, may smear, may or may not wash out, and may or may not fade in light. Use permanent fabric pens to sign quilts, add features to toy faces, identify clothing, or make other permanent visible marks. New products for quilters include pens or chalk pencils designed to fade intentionally within two to twelve days. Some of these are air erasable, some are water soluble, and some disappear chemically. It's best to design your work so markings will not show when it is completed.

THE DESIGN CENTER

This consists of a permanent floor and a portable wall leaning against a storage cupboard for fabrics (Fig. 4-9). To begin, I work flat, pulling out fabrics to try various colors and textures to see what looks best. Once these preliminary choices are made, pieces are taped or pinned partly assembled to the wall for better viewing. The wall is also good for photographing artwork.

Technique for Making a Foldable Pinning Wall

1. Materials: The materials you will need include two 4' x 8' (122cm x 244cm) pieces of Fome-Cor 1/2" (1.5cm) thick, 7' (213cm) of 2" (5cm) wide clear packaging tape, and 23' (701cm) of 1" (2.5cm) wide white masking tape. Fome-

ANGLES OF CIRCLES

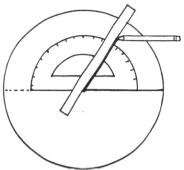

4-6. *Use a compass to make a circle or use a cardboard strip by tacking one end and rotating a pencil around it.*

CIRCLE

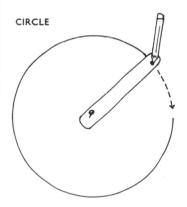

4-7. *To make angles, use a protractor marked in degrees. Measure the angle from a baseline point.*

4-8. *In the patterns for the games use the eighteen-degree angle to make the dart board sections, and use the sixty-degree angle for the Chinese checkers or the pattern given repeated twelve times in a star shape.*

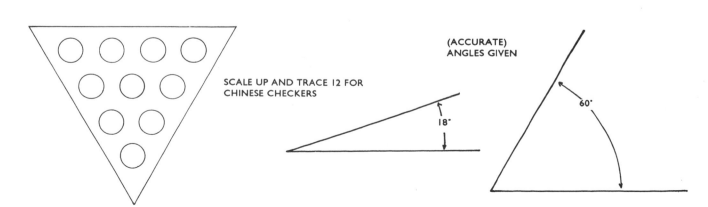

SCALE UP AND TRACE 12 FOR CHINESE CHECKERS

(ACCURATE) ANGLES GIVEN

18°

60°

4-9. The design center consists of a portable Fome-Cor wall to pin on, assorted fabrics to consider, and a chair for contemplating. Direction for making this wall are given. It can be stored under the bed.

Cor consists of a puffy plastic core covered with smooth white posterboard on each side and comes in various thicknesses.

1. Cut each piece 7' (213cm) long with a utility knife.

2. Stack the pieces, aligning the long edges exactly.

3. Using the 2" (5cm) clear tape, tape the length of the pieces along the edge. The center of the tape covers the crack and equal edges fold down onto the Fome-Cor (Fig. 4-10).

4. Stand the boards up and open them, keeping the taped edges held tightly together. Using white masking tape, tape over the joining of the two pieces in one strip, top to bottom, 1/2" (1.5cm) on each side of the seam. The white masking tape does not stick as securely as the package tape but it matches the surface better. The combination of it and the packaging tape is strong and unobtrusive.

5. Secure the tape hinge by taping across the top and bottom edges with white tape.

Sometimes, the art store will provide a clear plastic envelope wrapper. Use this to store the folded wall, and keep it under the bed or behind furniture.

2. Fabrics: Fabrics are bursting out of the storage cupboard shown in Fig. 4-9. Additional ones sit in boxes and baskets. Group fabrics according to your use, by type (such as cottons or wools), by color, by weaves, or by amounts. Give fabrics room to breathe in baskets or open crates, not crammed so tightly they mildew, as mine could without constant use. Every now and then, re-sort your collection and discard what you can. Parting will not be so traumatic if you have a garage sale, give them to a group that does crafts, or mail them to your mother.

3. Pins and Grippers: Pins and grippers come in a variety of sizes, shapes, and configurations. The Grabbit magnetic pincushion is a marvelous pin holder. Just drop the pin on or near it and—snap!—it's held. You can also run it over the floor to collect any spilled pins. T-shaped pins are handy to affix plans or fabrics to the bulletin board or to pin the quilt layers to the rug for "squaring up." Twist pins, used to hold chair covers in place, could also be used for this purpose.

THE CONSTRUCTION CENTER

A difficult thing to come by is a lovely big worktable that you need not waste time cleaning up daily. Mine consists of a piece of 4' x 6' (122cm x 183cm) plywood over file drawers and cupboards topped by a rotary cutting board with measuring grid. I also work on a counter to iron fusible webbing on appliqué pieces. The small ironing board (Fig. 4-11) used for applying fusible webbing to appliqués takes up minimum space and hangs inside a closet door.

Technique for Making a Light Box

The light box at the top left in Fig. 4-11 is useful for designing quilt squares, tracing images, aligning appliqués, drawing accurate seam lines on finished blocks, and viewing slides. You can use the T square along its edges for accurate straight lines and right angles. The box shown is a Seerite brand, but you can make your own (Fig. 4-12).

1. Materials: Assemble a clear plastic panel 16" x 20" (40.5cm x 51cm) or as desired, 6' (183cm) of 1" x 2" lumber—this actually measures 3/4" x 1-3/4" (2cm x 4cm), eight 1" (2.5cm) screws, eight 2" (5cm) finishing nails, two 15" (38cm) fluorescent or two incandescent fixtures, bulbs, and a power drill.

1. Saw the lumber into four pieces, two 20" (51cm) long and two 14-1/2" (37cm) long. Nail the longer boards to the ends of the shorter ones.

2. Attach the fixtures to the frame or simply set the box over them.

3. Drill holes at the edges of the plastic. Nails might split it. Screw the plastic to the top edge of the board frame.

2. Adhesives and Bonders: Adhesives and bonders make sewing and quilting easier. Most glues and adhesives stiffen fabrics and some glues bleed through or seep around the edges for unappealing results. To offset this, the products come in various forms: liquid glue to apply in controlled amounts, powdered heat-bonding glue to shake on like salt, tape that holds zippers and hems in place for sewing, a squeeze bottle to keeps fabric edges from fraying, and paper-backed rolls for making fabrics fusible. Several of these are water soluble for basting underlining, appliqué pieces, lace trim or similar tasks.

See chapter 7 for details on fusing fabrics for machine appliqué.

3. Cutting Tools: Buy the best quality you can. Good scissor blades have a slight inward curve so the blades mesh for their entire distance. This allows for making long, strong cuts by opening the blades wide or for making short snips from the tips. Never buy cheap scissors, even for children, who lack adult strength in their hands—cheap scissors are harder to use than good ones. Give young children kiddy scissors designed to cut paper only—not hair, clothes, tablecloths, or the cat's whiskers—then switch to 4" (10cm) round-tipped scissors of good quality and supervise their projects.

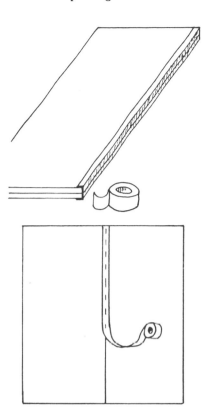

4-10. *Stack Fome-Cor pieces together, aligning the long edges exactly. Clear tape the length along the crack and fold the tape down onto the Fome-Cor. Open the boards and tape over the joining from top to bottom.*

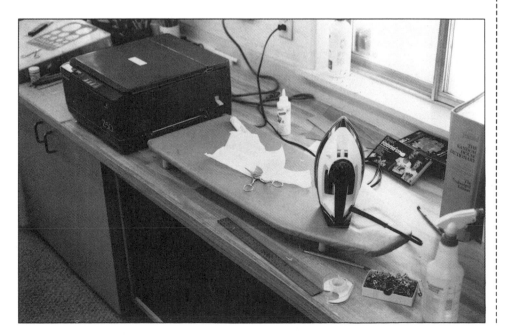

4-11. *On the "construction center" counter sits a portable ironing board, which I can store by hanging on a door, my husband's copier, and a light box at the top left with a circle-drawing guide on it.*

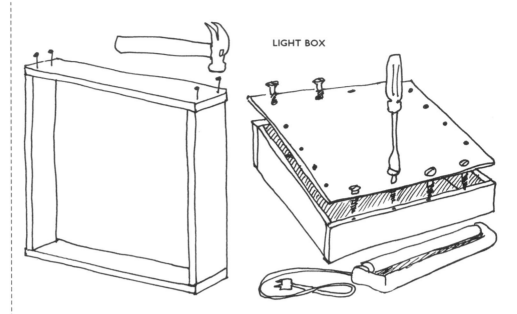

LIGHT BOX

4-12. *To make your own light box, nail together 1" x 2" lumber—actual size 3/4" x 1-3/4" (2cm x 4cm)—screw on translucent plastic, and affix under-the-shelf fluorescent lights inside.*

Here are some recommended cutting tools:

1. 7" (18cm) bent dressmaker shears

2. 4" (10cm) embroidery scissors

3. 6" (15cm) "duckbill" scissors with one wide blade for trimming the appliqué seam allowances

4. Utility shears for cutting leather, plastic, sandpaper, and so on

5. Rotary cutters in regular or industrial size and a cushioning pad

6. Utility knife

THE SEWING CENTER

1. Sewing Machines: Sewing machine preferences are based on the machine's abilities, cost, size, complexity, and other considerations. I use a mid-cost Kenmore for its wide bite (a zigzag stitch width), its embroidery stitches, and its manual settings. B. J. Adams uses a commercial Bernina-made machine for speed, strength, and type of stitch. The serger is used by some for strip quilting. If you want a new machine, try several first using your own fabric to see what they can do.

2. Needles: Keep a good supply of sewing machine needles on hand. Sometimes, the answer to a sewing problem means switching to a different type of needle to do a better job; see chapter 6 for more explanation.

Here are some recommended needle types:

1. "Sharp" needles cut through the fibers for the straightest stitch line.

2. "Ballpoint" needles push the fibers aside, causing a slightly offset stitch line but no runs or holes on knits.

3. "Top-stitching" needles have a deeper scarf or thread groove for thicker threads.

4. "Leather" needles have a wedge cutting point.

5 "Twin" or "double" needles, which are limited to most front-threading zigzag machines, make two perfect parallel rows on the top and a single zigzag row on the back.

3. Heat Press: The press on the chest to the right of the sewing machine is ideal for the fusing process in appliqué, for heat transfer of designs, and for steaming fabrics. The hand iron is better for pressing open seams because you can move it along a seam. Keep the face plates clean on either, especially when using the heat-setting fusibles. These stick to the iron and smear. Use Dritz Iron-off or a similar product to clean a dirty iron.

4. Storage: Threads are stored on the wall and in drawers. Use plastic drawers found in stationery stores for small notions. Use wooden chests for fusibles, machine manuals, tapes, or whatever you want close at hand. Spring-tension embroidery and quilting hoops hang on the door stop. Maintain a good light as you sew, whether by window light or by lamp. Get a magnifier to see clearly what you are doing. Buy a can of compressed air to blow the lint out of your machine as you sew or use a small battery vacuum for the same purpose.

Note: For good ideas on sewing supplies and how to use them consult sewing supply catalogs. Good catalogs include *Clotilde's Catalogue of Sewing Notions*, *Nancy's Notions*, and *Keepsake Quilting—the Quilter's Wish Book* (see Sources). Understanding your tools and how they work makes projects easier.

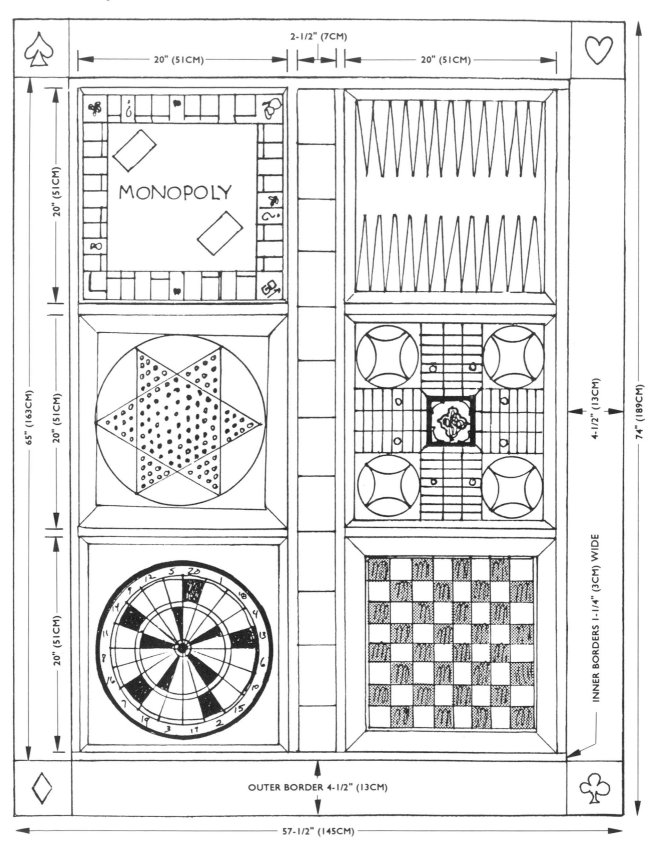

4-13. *Here is the pattern for the Game Quilt. Scale it up and then neaten and "true" the lines, circles, and angles with drafting equipment.*

PROJECT: CIRCLES AND SQUARES: GAME QUILT
(Fig. 4-13 and C-12 in the color section)

Overview: This quilt is made with a combination piecing, appliqué, and machine-embroidery techniques. The game board blocks are joined to sashing, a border forms the quilt face, and a blanket serves as filler and backing. If the complicated quilt seems too much to take on, do single game blocks for pillows.

Theme: The games featured are all old favorites, each generations old. Our family has played all of them with varying degrees of intensity over the generations. The realistic style comes from tracing the game boards, or using drafting tools to make the patterns. You can use different games by tracing the actual game board for a pattern and "true up" the lines as described above.

Techniques: Piecing, appliqué, reverse appliqué, machine embroidery, direct tracing of the pattern, and blanket backing.

Colors: The colors came from the game boards themselves, augmented with fabric designs and colors chosen to establish a mood of times past.

Size: The overall quilt 57-1/2" x 74" (145cm x 189cm); the Monopoly board: 19" (48cm) square, frame 1/2" (1.3cm); the Chinese checkers: 16" (41cm) circle on square, frame 2" (5cm); the dart board, the Backgammon board, and the Parcheesi board: 18" (45cm) circle on square, frame 1-1/4" (3cm); the chess board: 16" (40.5cm) grid, frame 1" (2.5cm); outer border: 4-1/2" (12cm) wide; inner borders: 1-1/4" (3cm) wide; and the center strip: 2-1/2" (7cm) wide.

Note: Dimensions given for fabrics in the listing below are for amounts of fabric needed and sometimes allow for cutting several pieces. These are not pattern-piece dimensions; for those consult the diagram measurements and add seam allowances.

MATERIALS

Note: Fabrics for this quilt were selected for color, texture, and surface design. They range from cottons through various mixes to polyesters and others, but all are a flat, tight weave. The piece is not intended to be washed. Use all cotton-polyesters for a washable quilt.

Monopoly block: Fabric amounts needed for cutting pattern pieces: 20" (51cm) square very light green (includes seam allowance); 3" x 6" (7.5cm x 15cm) each of light blue, plum, purple, blue, yellow, fuchsia, red, magenta, black and orange; outline threads in black and red; 6" x 24" (15cm x 61cm) navy for frame strips.

Backgammon block: Fabric amounts needed for cutting pattern pieces: 20" (51cm) square off-white; 8-1/2" x 24" (21.5cm x 61cm) deep gold, paisley-patterned rust, and purple (frame); outline threads in orange and red.

Chinese checkers: Fabric amounts needed for cutting pattern pieces: 18" (45.5cm) square light yellow; 9" (23cm) square medium blue; 5" (12.5cm) square of yellow, pink, red, orange, green, and rust; iron-on mending strip fabric in black, red, yellow, white, green, blue, and rust; outline threads in orange, red, golden brown, and lighter shades of iron-on colors; 16" x 24" (40.5cm x 61cm) gray-green frame.

Parcheesi Board: Fabric amounts needed for cutting pattern pieces: 20" (51cm) square of creamy white; four 7" (18cm) squares of golden brown, four 7" (18cm) circles of print, 1 yard (92cm) of 2" (5cm) wide ribbon, and 1/2 yard (46cm) of 1" (2.5cm) ribbon (cut from the border fabric); outline threads in red, black, and brown; 8" x 24" (20cm x 61cm) maroon frame.

Dart board: Fabric amounts needed for cutting pattern pieces: 20" (51cm) square of strip-patterned black, tan, and cream fabric; 19" (48cm) circle of black, 15" (38cm) circles of light green and gold, and 1" (2.5cm) red circle; 8" x 24" (20cm x 61cm) golden-brown frame.

Chess board: Thirty-two 3" (7.6cm) squares in various whites and taupes; thirty-two 3" (7.6cm) squares in various blacks and dark browns; 4" x 24" (10cm x 61cm) rust inner frame; 16" x 24" (40.5cm x 61cm) lavender and blue print frame.

Tools and supplies: Sewing machine, threads, sharp scissors, drafting tools including a ruler, a triangle, a protractor, a tack and cardboard or a compass, 20" (50cm) paper squares for patterns and stabilizer, paper-backed fusible webbing, and a pencil.

PROCEDURE

Techniques for Making a Pattern

To make a pattern, scale up the drawing as described in chapter 5. It is easiest to make individual 20" (50cm) square game patterns. Some parts are given full size, such as details of the Monopoly game, a triangle of the Chinese checkers board, and angles for dividing circles in sections. You can trace the games in reverse, sew through from the back for guidelines, and leave the paper in place as a stabilizer for stitching.

Note: If you plan to use different games, trace the game board and true the lines and then select appropriate fabric colors.

Technique for Making the Blocks

To make the blocks, consult the following related chapters for techniques:

1 Monopoly: satin-stitch embroidery through the pattern, chapter 6; "fused" appliqué, chapter 7.

2 Backgammon: "from the back" appliqué, chapter 7

3 Chinese checkers: "fused" appliqué, chapter 7; machine embroidery, chapter 6; use iron-on tapes for marbles with satin-stitch highlights.

4 Parcheesi: "through the pattern" appliqué, chapter 7; machine embroidery, chapter 6.

5 Dart board: "reverse" appliqué, chapter 7; machine embroidery chapter 6.

6 Chess/checkers: English or American piecing, chapter 3.

Technique for Assembling the Quilt Face

1 Complete the game boards so that with frames each measures approximately 20" (51cm) square plus 1/2" (1.5cm) seam allowances for a total of approximately 21" (53cm)(see Fig. 4-13).

2 Cut out inner and outer border pieces. Cut ten inner border strips 2-1/4" (6cm) wide. Cut all four outer border strips and four corner pieces 5-1/2" (14cm) wide.

3 For accuracy in stitching, measure and draw seam lines on the back of all pieces with a pencil and ruler. Match and pin the seam lines to sew the pieces together.

4 Assemble pieces in this order.
   Make two vertical strips by joining the Monopoly block to an inner border strip, to the Chinese checkers block, to an inner border strip, to the dart block. Next join the Backgammon block to an inner border strip, to the Parcheesi, to an inner border strip, to the checkers block. Make a third vertical strip by joining 12 blocks 3-1/2" (9cm) wide by 5-1/4" (13cm) long, total length 63" (156cm) including seam allowances.

Beginning on the left, join an inner border strip to the Monopoly strip. Add an inner border strip, the twelve-block vertical strip, an inner border strip, the Backgammon strip, and an inner border strip. Add an inner border strip to the top and bottom of this center panel.

Join outer borders on each side of the center panel. Sew a corner piece on each end of the top and bottom outer border pieces. Join these strips to the center panel to complete the quilt face.

Technique for Assembling the Layers

Select a firmly woven blanket of a good color, such as rust, peach, or tan. Lay the quilt face down on the blanket; pin and seam the edges, leaving an opening to turn. Trim the corners, turn, sew the opening closed, and hand or machine quilt. Leave the upper hemmed corners open for rod pockets (see Fig. 2-11).

5-1. *An appliqué portrait of* Little Red Riding Hood *measures 21" x 23-1/2" (53cm x 60cm). Reproduce this or make your own portrait using the project directions given at the end of this chapter.*

TRANSFER: MOVING PICTURES

Chapter Five

❖

W e live in a world full of images, those we see on our own and those brought to us by print and by photo, and by newspapers, magazines, books, posters, billboards, movies, video, and television. Why not use these images, save them, remodel them, transform them to our purposes? Moving visual messages from one place to another has become high-tech, and much of this technology is available to the art quilter at home. Still, sometimes the simple, direct techniques work best.

This chapter covers a range of ways to transfer images, along with the reasons for doing so: (1) to move the image to fabric for sewing; (2) to transfer the actual design by means of fabric paint, photo image, heat transfer, or other; and (3) to alter the image by reducing or enlarging it, by augmenting it, by adding details or combining images, or by simplifying it to suit fiber construction.

The project for this chapter, *Little Red Riding Hood* (Fig. 5-1), shows how to translate a photograph into an appliquéd stitchery. It was made using an Artograph projector, which will be described in the "Projecting Images" section, but other ways could have worked. Several techniques follow for transferring imagery.

TECHNIQUES FOR TRANSFERRING IMAGERY

Make a Freehand Drawing

This works fine if you draw well, and it has a certain primitive charm when you feel that you do not draw well. Doing your own drawing allows for personal interpretation; for consciously (or not) adding your opinion by the lines and shapes you choose. Success comes not so much by how well you draw as by how consistently your idea is carried out. Your goal is to create imagery on fabric the best way possible to tell your story.

When I asked my granddaughter, Hattie Stroud, to make pictures for a quilt for chapter 8 on color, she sat right down and began. Unfortunately, few of us draw as unself-consciously as a child, but you can borrow images, as many fiber artists do, either directly or as a basis for their images. This means you need not know how to draw "freehand" like Hattie, as much as you need to have a good design eye. It's the result that counts.

Using a Grid

Overlaying an image with a grid system is the most common way to graph it up (or down) to size. This technique requires little equipment and is fairly accurate. Almost any kind of imagery can be enlarged or reduced this way, such as a sketch you've drawn or artwork you've found. Cultural exchange is based on people borrowing ideas and images from each other, but do give credit if you borrow someone else's artwork. Often, artists who have based their work on another name their prints or paintings "Homage to (the artist's name)" because they respect the effort and insight that had gone into creating the borrowed image.

I. Materials: Have on hand an original image, paper the size of the completed pattern, a T square or drawing board with a sliding ruler, a pencil, and an eraser. Optional materials include acetate overlay, or India ink and a pen; see chapter 4 for instructions on making an accurate grid.

1. To enlarge or decrease the size of an image and create a pattern in the process, begin by making a grid over the original. If the original is disposable such as a sketch or a magazine picture, draw a grid on the image. Grid size is not important but accuracy is.

It helps to use gridded paper to start. Use lined notebook paper or graph paper to trace the image. For larger images, use tracing paper. For a reusable overlay, draw a grid in permanent ink on an acetate sheet, available in pads at art supply stores. Lay the grid over the artwork and tape it in place with removable masking tape (Fig. 5-2).

2. On paper the size of your pattern, draw a second grid with squares the size you need. If you plan to double the size of a drawing, make the grid squares twice as big. To reduce an image, make the second grid dimensions proportionally smaller than the original grid.

3. Use a pencil to transfer the design lines in the smaller square onto the larger square. Note where the lines cross grid lines. Do they intersect half way, a third of the way? Keep the eraser handy to correct mistakes. It may help to try a trick from chapter 1. Turn the original upside down to transfer it to the larger grid, and draw it upside down. This way, you aren't trying to draw what it is but how the pattern of lines fits in the grid. When you've finished, turn it right side up to neaten or correct the lines.

5-2. To enlarge an image, (a) overlay it with a grid; and (b) make a larger grid and reproduce the lines in each square.

A.

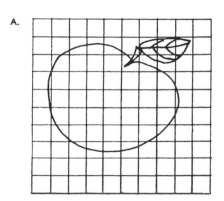

B.

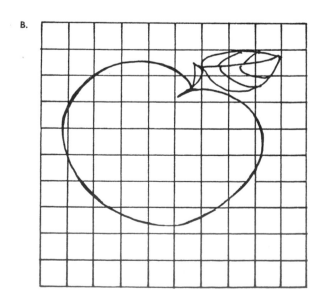

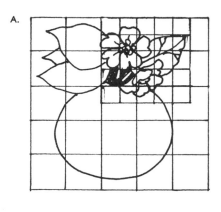

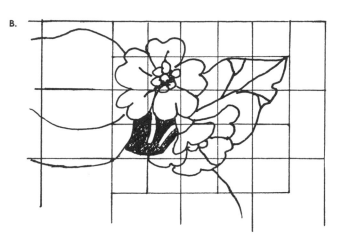

5-3. For a detailed area, (a) make a smaller grid within the overlay grid; and (b) make a grid to scale in the larger grid and copy the lines.

4. For very detailed areas, make a grid within a grid. Draw additional grid lines to a smaller scale within the square or area needed (Fig. 5-3).

5. Change the paper grid squares to rectangles for some inventive effects. If you want the image taller, make the squares in vertical rectangles; for a wider image try horizontal rectangles (Fig. 5-4).

6. Another way to use a grid is to draw your preliminary sketch on graph paper. Pads of this are available in art or office supply stores. This allows you to scale the sketch up (or down) readily. It also lets you figure out how much fabric you will need for various areas by counting squares.

Tracing

Tracing is a means of copying a drawing or photo by overlaying it with translucent material and following the lines.

1. Choose Thin Paper: Tracing paper, an ideal material for this, was created originally for architects and engineers for tracing plans. The heavier weight tracing and sketching paper is stronger and comes in drawing pads or rolls. Typing or copy paper, the least expensive and most useful paper to keep on hand, may show the image through it well enough for tracing if the original has a lot of contrast.

2. Use Removable Tape: Tape down the original with removable tape. Secure the tracing paper across the top only so you can flip it up to check details and lay it back down accurately

3. Light the Image From Behind: Use light behind the image if you cannot see the image well enough. Tape it on a window with daylight behind it, tape the paper over it, and trace. You can also use a light box to trace (chapter 4). If the image has something printed on the reverse side, this second image will make tracing confusing with a light behind it so try thinner tracing paper.

4. Trace by Sewing Machine: You can use your sewing machine to trace lines in several ways. (1) Trace lines from an original to paper by sewing through the original over the paper using no thread. Thus a perforated line results. (2) Lay the image over fabric carbon paper and sew with no thread to leave a dotted line tracing. (3) Pin a reverse image to the back side of the fabric and sew through, this time using thread.

A.

B.   RECTANGLE GRID

5-4. To elongate an image, (a) overlay it with a square grid; and (b) draw a rectangular grid and reproduce the lines from square to rectangle.

5-5. *To trace the outline of a three-dimensional object, silhouette it in a beam of light on paper and trace the shadow.*

Shadow Tracing

To trace a three-dimensional object, project a shadow onto the paper (Fig. 5-5). To do this, work in a darkened room. Use a lamp, such as a strong flashlight, and place it six or eight feet away. At the same level as the lamp, tape paper to the wall or stand a tracing pad on a table or stool. For exact-size imagery, put the object, such as the teapots in chapter 2, on the table touching the pad and then trace the shadow. To make a larger image, move the teapot away from the paper.

Pantograph

A pantograph is an instrument made of four light, rigid links joined in a parallelogram form, which is used to copy maps, plans, or other images on a predetermined scale. With this device, you draw the pattern with a pencil attached to the hinged arms by guiding the pantograph point around the image (Fig. 5-6).

PHOTOGRAPHY

In a flash a camera can record what the artist must take hours to do. The result is different, of course, and has its own limitations, but photography opens up a vast new kind of imagery for art quilts. Many of the artists in this book have incorporated photography in one way or another. Some of these ways follow.

Taking Photos for Quilting

Plan ahead when you take photographs to get the shots you need. To make the art quilt in chapter 3, I photographed several Victorian houses in town, looking for the right one to make into a pieced quilt pattern. Piecing works best with geometric shapes, so I aimed for straight-on shots. Taking several shots gave me choices later on; see the photos in chapter 3.

The overcast winter day softened shadows on the buildings, so for these low-light conditions, a fast film was needed. I used 400 ASA film (American Standards Association exposure index of light sensitivity). The noontime sun makes fierce contrast in photographs, so avoid it when possible. On bright days use a slower film with a 100 or 200 ASA for finer detail. I could have used a tripod to keep the camera still, but I was jumping in and out of my car so I didn't lug a tripod along. Photography balances the amount of light and shadow and the time it takes the light to expose the emulsion on the film.

5-6. *Trace the lines of the image and the pantograph enlarges it to the scale you choose.*

Once you capture the image you want, you can use photographs in combination with fabric. A variety of ways is described below.

Technique for Scaling a Photo into a Piecing Pattern

As an example, see the *Peabody House* in chapter 3; see also Fig. 5-7. The only materials you will need include a photo with simple geometric shapes, if possible, full-sized paper, and a ruler.

Begin by drawing a baseline that corresponds to the baseline of the house. Draw a vertical line for the left edge of the house. If you are lacking a right-angle triangle, use the corner of this book to measure.

Measure the total height of the house in your photo. If it comes to 4" (10cm) on your scale and you want a pattern 16" (40cm) tall, multiply the measured dimension by four, and mark the rooftop at 16" (40cm). Measure the photo house width, multiply by four, and mark this. Draw a vertical line on the mark for the right side. Put a mark up this line at 16" (40cm). This will make a box within which all measured and drawn lines will fit. If they don't, you've measured or multiplied incorrectly.

5-7. To make a geometric pattern of a house make a grid, measure the dimensions with a ruler, and draw the house on the grid. Draw the outside shape first and fill in increasingly smaller details as you draw. Square up shapes and simplify where you can.

Continue by measuring the next largest section, the eaves line, for example, and mark it, then the roof lines, then the overall porch size, or whatever details your house has. Details such as window sizes or trim widths will be difficult to measure, but by the time you get to them by working from large areas to smaller, you will have points to compare. Measure to see if all the windows are the same width and height, and what features line up with what other features.

There's a good chance your photo has some distortion from perspective. Eliminate this as much as possible to make your pattern as squared as you can. Leave some perspective in, such as the angles on the roof, so the shape of the building shows.

Photostating and Photocopying

Photostating is a photographic process for making an image scaled to almost any size you wish on photographic paper. Photostats can be made in reverse or on clear acetate sheets or can be half-tone screened for printing.

Photocopying, a different process, gives a quick reproduction in black and white or in color on paper. You can copy imagery from magazines, books, photographs, documents, or actual materials. Use the results to make patterns, reproduce the image several times for repeat patterns, change a slide to paper (with certain brands of color copier), or transfer the actual image to fabric.

Photo Transfer Gel

In this process, the actual photograph or photocopy is transferred to the fabric. Some types of paper work better than others, as noted on the label for the photo transfer gel named Picture This Transfer Medium for Fabric. Photocopies in black and white or in color are recommended because glossy pictures (especially plastic RC paper) may not work. The medium picks up the image and the paper backing is peeled off. A thin, soft paper will peel most easily.

This technique, like most, changes the hand of the fabric so that it has a thickened glaze on it. It also reverses the imagery, so use the face-up technique (see below) to avoid this. Unless you want unusual effects, apply the image to a layer of white or light fabric before applying it to a dark fabric. After transferring the photo, you can manipulate the fabric image by machine sewing, by adding decorations, by fabric painting, or by gluing on embellishments.

1. Preparation: Select your imagery and have it photocopied. Prewash the fabric to remove fillers or coatings and pin or tape the fabric (a quilt block, a T-shirt, or whatever) to a flat surface protected by papers or plastic sheeting. You can do this face down or face up.

2. Face-Down Technique: Trim the image to size and place it face up on waxed paper. Brush on a thick coat of the transfer gel medium and place the image face down on the fabric. Cover with a paper towel and use a rolling pin to press the image into the fabric. Remove the paper towel and let the fabric dry for twenty-four hours. Soak the paper backing with a sponge until it can be peeled off. Sponge off any residue of paper and let it dry. Seal the cleaned image with a second coating of the photo transfer gel.

3. Face-Up Technique: Place the image on waxed paper and apply a coat of the transfer gel medium, brushing in one direction. When it dries, apply another coat, brushing crosswise across the first coat. Let it dry for twenty-four hours.

Soak and then rub the paper backing off. Place the image face down on waxed paper and apply a coat of the transfer gel medium. Position the image face up on the fabric, cover with a paper towel and roll it smooth, as above.

Photo Emulsion on Fabric

This process requires a photographic darkroom if you do the steps yourself. Rosemary Reid collected 194 family pictures to make an heirloom quilt for her parents covering their forty years of married life (see C-13 in the color section). Fortunately, her father taught her photography so she could do the processing herself, which turned out to be a year-long project. A family quilt provided a basic design.

1. Rosemary chose to copy all the photographs and slides by camera so she would have negatives to work from and could control the size. Camera shops will do this for you, but with a good camera, a steady hand, and patience, you can do your own.

2. She used Liquid Lite Emulsion to coat the muslin quilt blocks for printing. This must be done in a darkroom under a red light. She brushed on two coats of emulsion, laid the squares on freezer paper, and stored the dried blocks in a lightproof box.

3. Back in the darkroom, Rosemary printed the fabric blocks by enlarger just as she would on photo paper. The blocks went into the developer, then into two fixing baths, and then were washed to make them permanent.

4. The fabric blocks were ironed flat and sewn into a quilt. This process results in a tough leathery surface on the fabric, not suitable for a usable quilt but fine for display.

Photo Screen Printing

Both artists and commercial fabric houses use screen printing to apply designs to fabric. This is a stencil process but has greater opportunity for fine detail than open stencils. For imagery, use a photograph or any other artwork that has been photostated onto a clear film. If the photo has gray tones, it will need to be half-toned—that is, made into patterns of various sized black dots, as are newspaper photos.

1. Lay the transparent photostat over a light-sensitive stencil film and expose it to a bright light to print the image.

2. Apply the exposed stencil film to a fine mesh fabric screen stretched taut in a frame and process by washing in cold water. Or the design image can be cut into a paper-backed acetate film and then applied to the screen. You can use water-soluble textile colors with the acetate screen but you will need oil-based colors for the water-soluble screen image so the image won't dissolve in printing.

3. The fine screen, originally silk or organdy but now made of synthetic fabric, allows textile paint to be squeegeed through the open design areas to print the fabric that is stretched taut on a flat surface.

4. Use a second screen to add a second color to the image. For yardage, screen-printed images are designed in an interlocking grid (see chapter 2; see also Fig. 5-8).

5-8. To screen-print, adhere a block-out stencil to a fine screen stretched in a frame. Pour in textile ink and squeegee to force the ink through the open parts of the stencil screen onto your fabric or paper.

Lori Bolt Hassled makes delightful screen-printed pillows in vibrant colors (see Fig. 2-4 in chapter 2). She often prints her designs on pre-printed fabrics as shown. Lori appliqués with satin-stitch outlining, decorative machine-stitching, and sewn-on objects. She and her family make their living as producing craftspeople selling at art fairs, so I can count on good craftsmanship and innovative ideas from her as I collect her pillows year after year.

Lori's mother, Sue Bolt, makes screen-printed graphics, known as serigraphs when screen-printed on paper. She's best known for her charming, colorful ceramic figures and tiles. Images on ceramic tiles can be screen-printed as well. Once you've picked up a technique, who knows how you will use it?

Marilyn Price uses screen printed imagery in her wall quilt *Summer Promise* (see C-14 in the color section). She screen-prints her images with textile dyes, colors that penetrate the fabric fibers and leave the quilt with a softer hand. She loads the screen with a range of colors, in this one from light blue to dark for a lovely graded color. Marilyn sets the color with steam heat, then quilts the layers to give dimension to the imagery by outlining them. She uses a variety of plain and fancy machine embroidery stitches for outlining.

In *Amigos* (see C-15 in the color section), also by Marilyn Price, she combines black-and-white photo screen-printed imagery with colorful leaves, birds, and colored quilted strips to show mixed realities.

Cyanotype or Blueprint

The cyanotype (from the Greek, meaning "dark blue impression") is one of the simplest and most permanent of all photographic processes. The action of ultraviolet light on exposed iron salt chemicals produces a vibrant blue background with a white negative image. Rinsing with water makes it permanent. Originally, architects' and engineers' blueprint drawings were made this way; now this is used only when archival quality is needed.

To blueprint on fabric, you need a full-size, contrasty image on clear film or a silhouette (as in the screen-printing process) to make a contact print on the light-sensitive fabric. This means you can print from a clear acetate photocopy, a Kodalith negative (a supercontrasty film), or found objects, such as lace, press-type letters, cutouts, flowers, or leaves. The image will be white and the

5-9. *Tafi Brown uses the cyanotype process for blueprinting photographic images on cotton fabric and then machine-pieces interlocking diagonal shapes into a wall quilt. This is the central panel of Coastal Maine, 28" x 43" (71.cm x 185cm).*

background blue. Only the Kodalith negative will make a "positive" image such as a portrait.

Tafi Brown is a photographer/artist who makes cyanotype wall quilts. She says, "The overall image one sees when looking at my work is a picture based on repetition of one or more photographic images although that is not immediately apparent. This visual duality or ambiguity fascinates me . . . the fact that I can take the familiar and change it to a new image that turns out to have much greater impact than the first image" (Fig. 5-9).

"Over the past fifteen years or so, I've made many quilts, the themes of which have often been timber farming. I make studio art quilts about things, times, places that hold importance for me and/or for other people," Tafi continues. "Recently, I've begun to do more 'painting with light'—that is, using photograms of actual objects in concert with through-the-lens photography" (Fig. 5-10).

Blueprint-Printables is a California company that provides pretreated white muslin squares for you to experiment on, saving you the effort of making your own light-sensitive fabric. To make your own chemical solutions, write to Photographer's Formulary, Inc., for blueprint chemicals or kits. See "Sources" for how to contact these firms.

Technique to Make Printed Fabric Squares

1. Work inside, out of bright light. Take out one sheet of treated fabric and reseal the black lightproof envelope. Pin or tape the fabric to a foam board so it is truly flat.

2. Use a contrasty film or silhouetted object and arrange it or whatever you are going to print on top of the square. Don't take longer than ten minutes to set up your design.

3. Cover the print with glass to keep it in contact with the fabric or affix a three-dimensional object with hidden pins so it won't blow off during exposure. Don't get the fabric wet or, if you are using live plants as imagery, stained with plant juice.

5-10. *Lately, Tafi Brown has been cyanotype-printing pine boughs, flowers, and other objects directly on fabric to make photograms. B. W. and Company On Pratt Road, 55" x 76" (140cm x 193cm), is pieced and appliquéd with cyanotype and photogram prints and commercial and hand-dyed fabrics.*

4. Print only on bright sunny days between 9 A.M. and 2 P.M. Expose the sandwiched print to the direct sun (no shadows) for about ten minutes. Use test strips first to determine the proper exposure.

5. Take the print inside and rinse it in cool water until the water is clear. Lay it on clean paper towels to dry.

Assemble these as you would any other fabric into a quilt.

PROJECTING IMAGES

The Opaque Projector

The overhead or opaque projector does away with the need to use a grid for scaling up or down. Use the Magnajector from Rainbow Industries, an inexpensive unit made for kids and hobbyists, in which a one hundred–watt bulb inside reflects the image on a mirror and through the lens to project on the wall. A more elaborate unit by Artograph has a larger image area, a sharper lens for a clearer image, and a cooling fan. Extras include a stand to hold the unit above your desk and a reducing lens.

1. To use the opaque projector, work in a room that can be darkened.

2. Locate the projector on a flat surface near a wall outlet. Aim it at a smooth wall at a convenient height for you to trace. Don't trip over the extension cord while you try to trace.

3. Select a large enough white sheet of paper, measure and mark on it the size you want the image to be, and tape the paper to a smooth wall.

4. Project and focus the image by moving the projector back and forth until it fits within your measured marks.

5. Trace the necessary lines. The larger you project the image, the more blurred the outlines will be. Before moving your setup, turn up the lights to see your results and make corrections.

6. If the image is larger than the viewing area, move the image to expose a new area, align the new image with the tracing, and complete the tracing.

Slide and Enlarger Projecting

Using a slide projector works the same as an opaque projector in your setup except that your original image exists in slide form. Use a darkened room and tape the paper to the wall in a convenient spot to work. Project the slide image on the paper and trace the parts you want. If you are starting with film negatives or positives and have access to an enlarger, use this to focus the image clearly just the size you want.

Margaret Cusack uses the above techniques to create her illustration (see C-16 in the color section).

5-11. *Here is the pattern for Little Red Riding Hood. Use this or make a pattern from your own photograph. The directions follow in Fig. 5-12.*

PROJECT: PHOTO PORTRAIT, *LITTLE RED RIDING HOOD*

(Fig. 5-11; and C-17 in the color section)

Overview: This project begins with a photograph and simplifies it into flat color areas of fabric. Fabric pieces are adhered with fusible webbing to the background and are machine satin-stitched in place. This sewn line also highlights the design.

Theme: Making a portrait by reducing subtly molded shadows to flat tones.

Techniques: (1) Transferring the image in increased size by opaque projector; and (2) making an appliqué fabric portrait from a photograph.

Size: Overall piece 21" x 23-1/2" (53cm x 59.5cm); center panel 11" x 13-1/4" (28cm x 33.5cm).

MATERIALS

Fabric amounts needed for this specific portrait: frame; 2/3 yard (61cm) brown velvet, white background fabric 21" x 23" (53cm x 58.5cm), 2-1/4 yards (231cm) of 3/4" (2cm) wide gold trim, 2 yards (183cm) of 1-1/2" (4cm) wide green pin-dot ribbon, 2 yards (183cm) of 1-1/2" (4cm) wide red print ribbon, navy background 12" (31cm) square, red 12" (31cm) square, warm brown 6" x 10" (15cm x 26cm), blue print 7" x 12" (18cm x 31cm), medium blue 3" x 4" (8cm x 10cm), blue smaller print 3" x 4" (8cm x 10cm), dark pink 3" x 7" (8cm x 18cm), flesh color 4" by 12" (10cm x 31cm), white collar 2" x 4" (5cm x 10cm), maroon 2" x 4" (5cm x 10cm), and gold fabric 3" x 7" (8cm x 18cm); threads in blue, pink, rust, dark brown, gold, ocher, maroon, red, and gold metallic; and paper-backed fusible webbing.

Tools and supplies: Sewing machine, paper for pattern, parchment paper, opaque projector, markers, tape, and scissors.

PROCEDURE

Make the Pattern

1 Follow the directions for using an opaque projector to scale up the pattern (Fig. 5-12), scale it up by grid, or trace your own choice of photograph. Directions follow for making your own photograph.

2 Carefully record each necessary line or shape. Increasing the size may make the image blurry so make the best choices of line placement you can under the circumstances.

3 If you are making a portrait from your own photograph or from a sketch of a person, analyze it for changes in color caused by shadows. Project the image again and draw the lines as best you can to indicate where shadows divide. Use shading to indicate the shadowed areas. Adjust your drawing until it looks right.

One easy way to reduce color nuances is to run your original color photograph or drawing through a black-and-white photocopier to change it to black-and-white values.

5-12. To make your own pattern, project the image by opaque projector (or scale up, as described). Draw lines where shadows begin—as best you can decide—and shade these areas.

Choosing Colors

Use markers or crayons to indicate what color each area should be or work from the original as a color guide. Select suitable fabric colors for each area. Shadow colors are hard to determine, so be inventive.

Lay out your fabric color choices so they match the required areas and relate to each other. Choose the fewest tones possible so it won't get too complicated. For example, the dress has a sky-blue print fabric and a darker gray-blue shadow. The red cape is shadowed with maroon. The pale peach face is shaded with muted orange.

Finding good face colors is difficult. Golden brown, which became the hair and basket, was not pink enough, and the pink I used was too pink, but it was the closest I could come without making a trip to the fabric shop. You can go with a close color and make it work by the choices of thread color added later.

Even a shopping trip may not produce the fabric color you want because of style and seasonal changes. Old clothing from a secondhand store or rummage sale may work better. Some stitchers dye their own. Best for shadow tones is to dye the facecolor fabric darker; see chapter 8 on color for more on this.

Make the Fabrics Fusible (see chapter 7 for details)

1 Reverse the pattern, place it on a light source, and outline the color area shapes. Lay paper-backed fusible webbing over the pattern and trace each shape separately on the smooth paper side. (The rough side is the webbing side.) Trim, leaving a border 1/4" (6cm) around each pattern piece to allow for overlap, to make sure the edges are adhered, and to get a neatly trimmed edge.

2 Lay the appropriate color of fabric face down on parchment paper. Align the fusible webbing paper pattern and iron it on. Leave the backing paper in place until you plan to fuse the appliqué piece.

Adhere the Fabric Appliqué Pieces

1 Iron fusible webbing on the back of the background fabric. To add appliqué fabrics, trim the webbing-backed pattern along the edge, leaving a narrow seam allowance on the under fabric for overlap where the colors meet. Peel off the paper and iron in place, using the lightbox or pattern as a guide.

2 Apply large areas first, adding smaller areas to overlay larger ones, such as the dress shadows over the dress fabric. These later pattern pieces will be trimmed exactly to size because they are not overlapped by another fabric (Fig. 5-13).

3 If a fabric shows an under color through it, fuse it to a white fabric or another color first.

Satin-Stitch Outline the Appliqué Pieces

Set your machine to satin-stitch and use matching thread or clear thread on the bobbin. Use contrasting thread colors to show outlines, add colors, and bring out fabric colors. Use thread that matches the appliqué pieces to diminish outlines. For more details on the fused appliqué process, see chapter 7 on appliqué.

Complete the Picture

1 Align the completed panel and ribbon framing on a background fabric, brown velvet as shown, and top-stitch the ribbons in place.

2 Draw accurate seam lines on the back of the velvet, align it with backing fabric, and seam the edges, leaving an opening to turn.

3 Trim the corners and turn. Press the edges from the back side. Hand stitch the opening closed. Top-stitch 1/4" (6mm) from the edge to finish.

5-13. To appliqué the portrait, fuse on large fabric areas first and then add smaller fabric patch details. Satin-stitch the pieces in place. For the finished portrait, see Fig. 5-1.

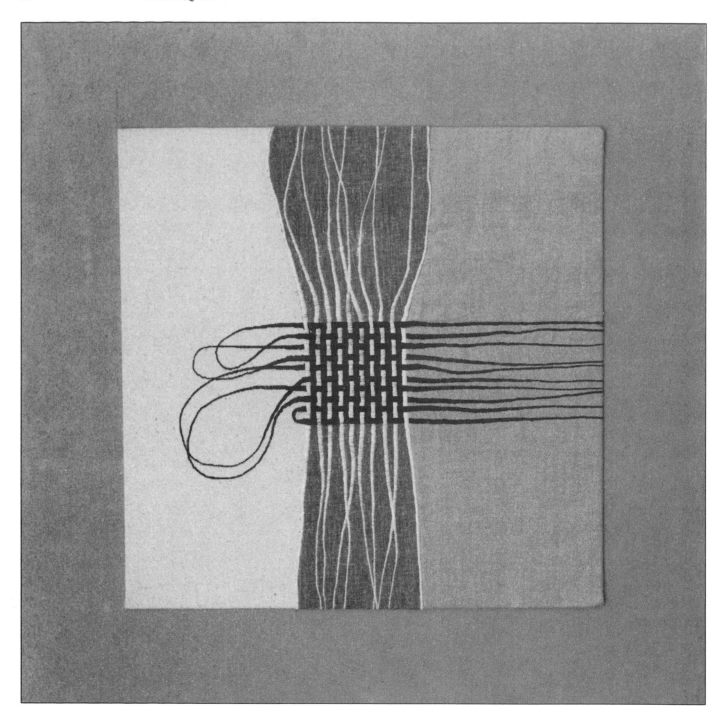

6-1. Interweave 24" (61 cm) square, one
of a series of machine-sewn embroideries
using machine satin-stitch to "draw"
yarns on fabric. To try this, see the
project at the end of the chapter.

LINES: EMBROIDERING
Chapter Six

L ines are an integral part of stitchery. They ramble across the surface in orderly or random designs, embellishing the fabric in a variety of ways, such as embroidery or applied designs. Lines make up the fabric itself because the interwoven threads are always apparent, no matter how finely woven, knitted, knotted, or crocheted the fabric. This, in part, is why many art quilters call themselves fiber artists: they work with fibers to make art.

This chapter details hand- and machine-embroidery techniques. The imagery is accomplished by the use of technique, so think of your thread as a line drawn by colored pencil on paper. That was my mind-set as I made *Interweave* (Fig. 6-1), and *Mesh* (see C-18 in the color section). In this series of ten pieces, my aim was to draw fibers with stitches showing the natural way they loop and drape. It appealed to me to be making machine embroidery about a drawing technique based on woven fibers. Try this yourself in the project for this chapter.

HAND EMBROIDERY

Before the advent of radio and television, rainy days in the country could be spent stitching embellishment on linens, clothing, and samplers. In those days, Mary Hall, my husband's mother, bought designs to iron on muslin squares for her children to embroider. These squares, which recently came to us, were combined with a vintage design fabric from the Pennsylvania Dutch country and were assembled into the Hall family quilt (see C-19 in the color section). My husband can't remember which he sewed, but he is certain the neatest is his.

Designs of this type are returning for sale in craft catalogs and stores, but you can make your own. With an iron-on transfer pencil, you can draw or trace a design on a piece of paper and then with a warm iron, transfer it to fabric. It reverses, remember. The Hall family quilt employs only an outlining stitch but you can design yours to use any and all stitches you wish, whether by hand or sewing machine. Information on these stitches follows.

Hand-Embroidery Stitches

The familiar stitches shown have been around so long and used in so many countries that they have multiple names, but the following are the most common. The first five are straight stitches. The next five are loop stitches in which the thread loops around another stitch. Any others are combinations of these two methods of forming stitches (Fig. 6-2).

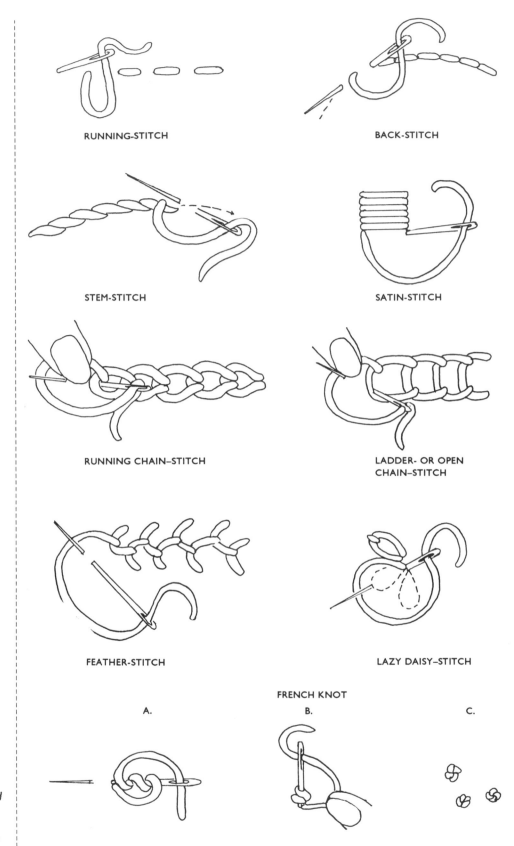

RUNNING-STITCH

BACK-STITCH

STEM-STITCH

SATIN-STITCH

RUNNING CHAIN–STITCH

LADDER- OR OPEN CHAIN–STITCH

FEATHER-STITCH

LAZY DAISY–STITCH

FRENCH KNOT

A.   B.   C.

6-2. *These are the basic, common embroidery stitches that can be combined to make endless other stitches. Consult the text for directions on making stitches.*

1. The running-stitch is a simple straight stitch. Do it one stitch at a time or in a row by bunching several stitches on the needle and then pulling it through. Done with sewing thread, this stitch is used to join seams and to quilt layers together. With embroidery thread, it is used to form single short lines or to fill in an area of color.

2. The back-stitch makes a solid line, a filled-in running-stitch. To do this, make a running-stitch that comes up a stitch length along the line. Sew back through the end of the last stitch and come up through the fabric the length of a stitch past the end of the second stitch. Repeat.

3. The stem-stitch looks like the underside of the back-stitch. Sew a stitch and come up halfway back on this stitch. Sew a stitch half-again as long as the first and come up halfway back on this stitch, which will be even with the end of the first stitch. The Hall family quilt is sewn with this stitch since it "draws" a solid line following the design. Also see the king's arm and sword for this stitch (Fig. 6-3).

4. The satin-stitch is an even row of straight stitches sewn side by side to form a solid line, satiny in appearance. This satin-stitched line will be as solid on the back as on the fabric face. The king's cuff is satin-stitched. The stitch also can be used to fill in shapes as on the Chinese crane's chest (Fig. 6-4).

5. The running chain-stitch is a loop stitch. To do this come up through the fabric and loop the thread ahead. Insert the needle in the same hole in which you came up, emerging a stitch length ahead inside the loop of thread under the point of the needle. Pull the stitch firmly to form a chain link and repeat. This stitch appears in Mary Gentry's *Quilt* on the robot's arms (see C-21 in the color section).

6. The ladder-stitch as a variation of the chain but is worked wider. The chain is opened up into a square-cornered U instead of a loop O. Come up through the fabric and loop the thread ahead. Insert the needle parallel with same place you came up but the width of the ladder away. Emerge a stitch length ahead catching the loop, but don't pull tightly. Repeat this step by inserting the needle parallel with the second stitch, the width of the ladder away and pull the stitch tight. Repeat.

6-3. *This detail (above) of the King (below) by the author shows stem-stitch.*

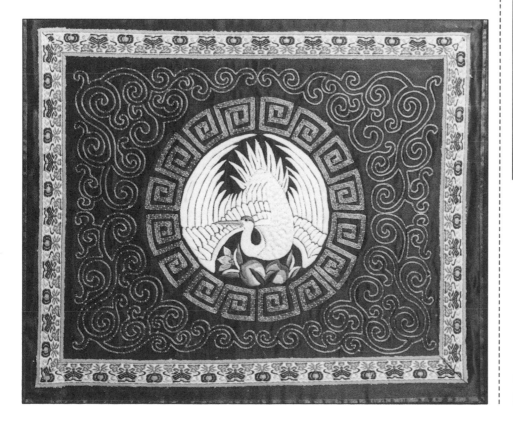

6-4. *This Chinese embroidery features a bird sewn in an intricate satin-stitching*

7. The lazy daisy–stitch is made like the chain-stitch except the links are formed around a center or however needed. Come up through the fabric with the needle, lay down a loop, and enter the fabric through the same hole, emerging a stitch away within the loop. Pull the stitch tight and enter the fabric on the outside of the loop. This stitch appears on the king's letter K (see Fig. 6-3).

8. The feather-stitch branches off from a center line like a feather. Sewn solidly this stitch fills in areas, since more thread lays on the face than on the underside of the fabric. To form this stitch, sew a long straight stitch at an angle and, before pulling it firmly in place, emerge to the side in the center of the first stitch. Pull up on the thread looping the first stitch around the base of it. Continuing forward, make a long stitch to the left side and catch it with the emerging needle for a second loop stitch. The next long stitch goes from left to right; the following right to left; and so on (Fig. 6-2).

9. Also on the king's robes is the French knot. For this, come up through the fabric, place the needle tip across the emerging thread, and then coil the thread around the tip three times (more or less). Pull the thread firmly to tighten and then push the needle through the coiled thread into the fabric to form the knot.

10. Couching is done by laying a large, decorative, or fragile thread on the surface and sewing it in place with another thread, as in the gold thread in the background of the crane and the key design (Fig. 6-4).

Just as in drawing with a pencil, stitch configuration need not be limited to a standard shape or named stitch. Make up your own by combining stitches and sewing one over another. Inspect a crazy quilt to see how many combinations those creative quilters in the 1890s devised.

Sewing Tools and Supplies

1. Embroidery Threads: Among other factors that make a difference in the quality of your work is the thread you use. Mary Gentry's pieces (see C-21 and C-28 in the color section) show a soft, loosely twisted thread called embroidery floss. It comes in small skeins in hundreds of colors, all listed by DMC brand or Anchor brand number so you can match your needs. Embroider with all six strands for fast coverage, or use fewer strands by pulling one or two loose. Expert Mary Zdrodowski says you get better coverage using one strand and more stitches.

Pulling strands can make a tangled mess, so you may wish to wind the floss on a flat "spool" card first. If not, pull out a sewing length of 15" (38cm) or so from the skein without tangling the remaining floss. Clip this off and hold the six strands between your index finger and thumb. Select one strand and pull gently to extract it. Pull another if you want to sew with two strands. The floss will bunch up and then fall back when single strands are removed. Embroidery floss comes in low-luster cotton thread, in high-sheen rayon or silk threads, and in soft-textured wool (for crewel embroidery). These threads will not fit through a sewing machine needle, although some can be used in the bobbin at times.

To hand sew seams and quilt layers together use a finer sized thread. Best for this is a firmly twisted thread of long-staple Egyptian cotton that is color-fast, light-fast, and won't shrink. You want a thread that won't loop and twist on itself, snarling your stitches. Better threads have eliminated the need for quilters to wax threads for trouble-free hand sewing, but get a beeswax plug if you need it.

2. Needles: Hand-sewing needles come in a wide variety since no needle is perfect for every task. If it is thin and easy to pull through the fabric layers, it is impossible to poke the thread through its tiny hole. If it's short enough for the mandated twelve stitches per inch in hand quilting, it's not long enough for quick basting. Here's a general listing of hand-sewing needle types. In sizing, the higher the number, the shorter the needle; thickness of hand-sewing needles decreases as size number increases.

Sharps, #11 and #12: A short (1-1/4" [3cm] or 1-1/8" [2.75cm] thin needle with a small eye for appliqué and quilting.

Betweens, from #9 to #12: Size #9 has a larger eye for easier threading.

Embroidery/crewel, sizes #5 to #10: a general needle (and my favorite), with a long eye for easier threading.

Tapestry (assorted sizes): a blunt needle with a long eye for open mesh materials.

Doll needle: a very long, coarse needle (3-1/2" [9cm] to 5-1/2" [14cm]) for sewing through thickness to anchor eyes or soft-sculpture faces.

Glover's/leather needle: has a triangular wedge point for piercing without tearing.

Needle threaders: come in superfine wire for threading most needles, a necessity for fraying threads or woolly nylon serger thread.

3. Thimbles: Thimbles to protect fingers from needle pricks were traditionally made of metal in various sizes. Now leather thimbles or open plastic finger guards may suit you better. I never could learn to use a metal thimble, always holding that finger apart as if it were injured. My leather thimble has a metal tip to push the needle through. Use a thimble or guard on either hand as you hand quilt.

Sometimes, you'll need a needle grabber, such as a leather patch, a doctor's hemostat, pliers, a flat balloon, or any handy device that gets a good grip on the needle to tug it through. Look for these in sewing supply books (see "Sources"). They show a fascinating array of devices to aid in hand sewing, from floss winders through magnifiers to mechanical needle threaders.

4. Hoops: No matter how good you become at hand sewing, it still pays to use a hoop when embroidering or quilting, to hold the fabric drum-tight for even stitching. Hardwood or plastic hoops come in several sizes, from 4" (10cm) to 12" (30cm) or more, and in different shapes, from round to oval. Don't leave the hoop on between sewing sessions, or overnight, for example, or it will leave indelible ring marks. Also be sure you sew with clean hands since hoop marks and grime are hard to remove.

5. Fabrics: Cotton and linen in firmly woven fabrics are traditional backgrounds for embroidery, but you can embroider on almost anything, including paper or plastic grid. Each fabric presents its pleasures and problems. You'll have to experiment with various needles, threads, and fabrics to see what works.

Double knits, velveteens, and polyester broadcloths are often too tightly woven to pull the threaded needle through. You'll find these tiring and frustrating to hand embroider; see chapter 9 for more about fabrics.

MACHINE EMBROIDERY

Hand-sewing to the evening television news is enjoyable, but my favorite technique is machine embroidery. In no time, I've got the machine up to full speed, building up layers of colors until the needle refuses to pierce the fabric one more time or the thread slices off. I've resisted buying a programmed electronic model sewing machine. I've heard they are incredible, but so far, I prefer to control the stitch width, length, and pressure on the presser foot myself as I sew. Also, they cost a mint.

Whatever machine you own, even a sixty-year-old straight stitch machine, can embroider by attaching a spring embroidery foot and using a hoop to hold the fabric taut (set the stitch length to zero). Realistically, a zigzag machine is imperative for satin-stitch embroidery. If you are looking for a new machine, investigate what each does first. Some art quilters choose industrial model machines to sew multiple layers, for speed, or for special skills such as embroidery, quilting, chain-stitching, couching, or other. B. J. Adams uses a commercial machine with a wide zigzag for her creations (see C-20 in the color section).

Read such sewing publications as *Threads*, *Quilter's Newsletter*, and *Sew News* for evaluation of various models (see "Sources"). When you get a machine, keep it oiled as per the manual, and keep it clean and free of lint.

How the Machine Works

If you know how a sewing machine forms a stitch, you won't get so angry at the machine for doing mysterious things. Sewing machines interlock two threads, one from the bobbin and the other from a spool on top. The top thread goes through guides and controls before going through the needle. First is a tension disk that controls the feed of the thread. Second is the take-up lever that pulls the thread back up after the needle takes it down to the bobbin. A bobbin hook spins around the bobbin, looping the top thread around the bobbin thread to form the stitch (see Fig. 6-5).

If the thread pulls out of the needle when you begin to sew, the take-up lever is on the up swing cycle, doing its job to keep the tension of the stitching even. Leave a tail of thread to prevent this. In machine embroidery you will have controls for these: thread tension, presser-foot pressure, and stitch length and width. Many machines do all this automatically, but I like the results of manipulating these few controls myself.

Important note: Read your machine manual and, if possible, take a basic sewing class.

1. The Tension Control: This keeps the thread feeding evenly and balances the stitches. A balanced stitch shows only the thread on that side of the fabric. Many embroidery stitches use an unbalanced stitch where the decorative top thread shows and the utility bottom thread does not. Threads vary in thickness and sheen, so they all require an adjusted tension. Sew a line of stitches, adjust the tension, sew, and re-adjust until you have what you want.

The take-up lever works with the tension control to keep the stitching even. The presser-foot lever also works with the tension disks, disengaging them when it raises the foot, so you can pull thread through as needed.

Machine manufacturers say to leave the bobbin tension screw alone as much as possible so that at least one tension control is consistent. Many machine embroiderers adjust it at will or have a second bobbin case. If you use a variety of

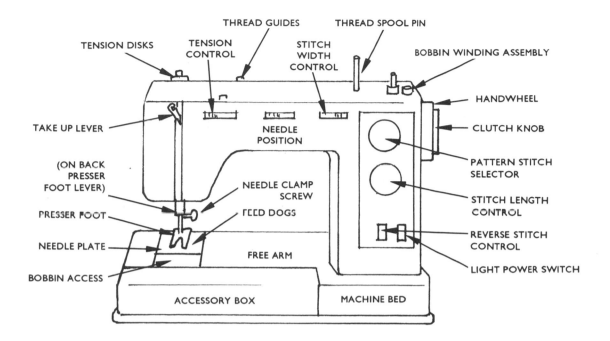

threads, including thick ones on the bobbin, learn how to adjust this control by reading your manual and by experimenting.

2. *The Stitch Width and Length Controls:* The width dial or lever controls the side swing of the needle. Use this for zigzag-stitching, satin-stitching, or other programmed stitches. The project describes using this while satin-stitching for a graceful-shaped line.

The stitch length indicator controls the feed dogs. The farther they move the fabric, the longer the stitch. Control this while sewing to get a tight or open zigzag stitch. It also alters the shape of programmed pattern stitches. For free-motion stitching, move this to zero or lower or cover the feed dogs altogether.

3. *The Pressure Control:* This applies pressure to the presser foot to hold the fabric down to form the stitch and keep the fabric in contact with the feed dogs in order to move ahead. On my machine, I can diminish the pressure for thicker fabrics and loosen it to "darn" for free-motion stitching. If this doesn't work on your machine, you can use an embroidery foot or spring attachment.

To Machine Embroider

1. *Threads:* A machine sewing thread must be strong and smooth enough to pass through the needle many times before it becomes a stitch. The take-up lever pulls it up and down, while the tension disks retard its free flow, and this is abrasive on threads. Rayon, silk, or metallic threads are especially apt to shred, but they are so handsome that they're worth the hassle.

Sulky has a particularly marvelous range of embroidery threads of shining colors, including metallics and variegated. They come on small tube-style spools cross-wound to keep them from falling off the spool. I've got a drawerfull of these fine colors that I dip into as if using a palette of paints (Fig. 6-6).

6-5. Sewing machines aren't magic, even though it would seem so. This diagram of a typical sewing machine shows how the stitch forms and where the controls are located.

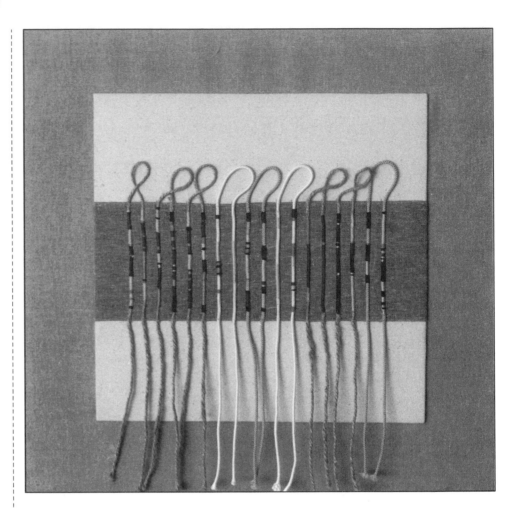

6-6. Rayon and silk threads are used to machine-couch ropes in place on Simulated Wrap, 24" (61cm) square, another machine embroidery in a series by the author.

Regular sewing thread, usually a blend of cotton and polyester, is tightly twisted for strength and does not cover as well in satin-stitching as the softer embroidery threads. A clear monofilament thread finer than the top thread is ideal for the bobbin thread in embroidery. It can be used on top for in-the-ditch quilting.

Use quality threads for the best results.

2. Needles: Sometimes sewing problems mean switching to a different size or type of needle to do a better job. Keep a good supply of sewing machine needles on hand. Match the needle to the thread, using the smallest-size needle that suits. Match the needle type to the fabric. "Sharp" machine needles cut right through the fibers for the straightest stitch line. "Ballpoint" needles push the fibers aside causing a slightly offset stitch line but no runs or holes on knits. "Top-stitching" needles have a deeper thread groove running up the back of the needle to accommodate thicker threads. "Leather" needles have a wedge cutting point. "Twin" or "double" needles (limited to most front-threading zigzag machines) make two perfect parallel rows on the top and a single zigzag row on the back.

Problems may mean that the needle is dull or has a bent tip. Change the needle if you are having trouble sewing, or are using different threads. Needle-lube, a silicone lubricant, helps eliminate skipped stitches from friction heat and static electricity. Sometimes, when the machine won't sew, it's enough to pull out the top thread and rethread through all the controls.

3. Hoops, Stabilizers, and Fusibles: The pull of the stitches is greater than the stiffness of most fabrics and will pucker them. Machine tensions can be loosened only so much and still form a stitch, so you must offset this tendency to pucker by other means. One is a spring-tension machine embroidery hoop for embroidery work. Machine hoops must be thin enough to slide under the presser foot. Sizes range from 6" (15cm) in metal and plastic with pinch handles to 12" (30cm) in wooden ones.

Even this may not be enough to avoid puckering. I usually use copy paper on the back of the fabric as a temporary stabilizer. For a soft hand, avoid a permanent stabilizer, such as fusible webbing. If it is more important that the stitchery remain smooth, use a fusible webbing that bonds the top layer of fabric to another; (see chapter 7 for more details).

Machine Stitches:

Technique 1: Straight stitch: Ordinary machine stitching in a straight line may be exactly right to create your imagery. In Erma Martin Yost's *Spirit Pass* (see C-1 in the color section) the silver lines look like rain. Below the horned animal the stitched line resembles distant peaks. When the peaks are filled in they gain solidity.

To straight-stitch as embroidery, stabilize the fabric, as mentioned above and set the machine for ordinary stitching. Test each different thread for the necessary tension setting and/or use monofilament thread in the bobbin. Sew forward as desired and then push the reverse lever. If your machine has no reverse setting you will need to stop sewing with the needle down, raise the presser foot to pivot the fabric, and then stitch.

Simple as this stitch is, it can be varied several ways. You can use a loose bobbin thread that is pulled up by a tighter strong top thread to whip over it. You can put two threads through the needle for mixed colors or use variegated thread for changing color.

Technique 2: Zigzag and Satin-stitch: Perhaps the most common machine-embroidery stitch is the satin-stitch. It can outline an appliquéd shape or give a wider line of color than the straight-stitch. Satin-stitching is used to draw straight and curved lines on *Mesh* by the author (Fig. 6-7 and see C-18 in the color section) and in the project.

Practice this stitch on a fabric identical to the one you plan to sew on to see if your fabric needs stabilizing. Set your machine for zigzag stitching. Loosen the top thread tension so that it shows on the back. Use a strong thin thread on the bobbin, such as monofilament, so it won't show on top and so you won't need to rewind the bobbin as often. Wind several bobbins. Set the stitch width to what you want, avoiding the widest setting since it will probably pucker the fabric. Set the stitch length to be very short. You'll need to test different settings to get it just the way you want. Use an embroidery thread for best coverage.

Use a satin-stitch presser foot that will clear the thickened row of stitching. It has a grove on the bottom for this. If you plan a lot of twists and turns, try reducing the pressure on the presser foot one step. When the sample stitching meets perfection on your practice fabric, switch to the real thing. Any problems you might incur will come at corners or in thread buildup that's hard to sew over. Overlap the sewn line on corners, or pivot carefully on round ones to maintain coverage.

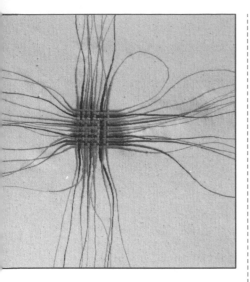

6-7. *You can pretend the sewing machine is a pencil and you are drawing in thread. This detail of* Mesh *by the author, from her series, shows how satin-stitched lines simulate weaving.*

6-8. *Zigzag stitching not only attaches the appliqué kitten and outlines it (from* Favorite Cats, *Fig. 9-1 in chapter 9) but the stitching makes stripes and features on mohair loop fabric.*

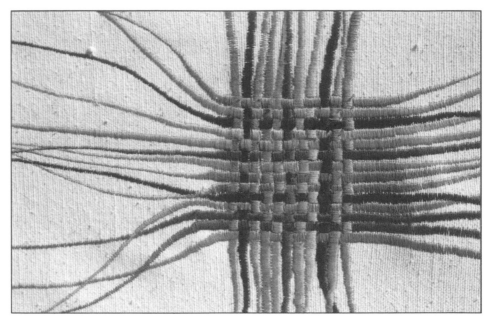

Technique 3: Satin-Stitch Fill In: For this stitch, set the machine the same as for satin-stitch. To change the width of the lines as you sew, guide the fabric with your left hand and move the stitch width control with your right. If this proves impossible with your machine, stop sewing and adjust the width as often as needed. B. J. Adams used this technique on *Bungy Attitude* (see C-20 in the color section) to create the dizzying effect that leaping off and stopping short on the bungee cord gives. She painted the design on canvas first in a bewildering array of colors and then selected vibrant, lustrous threads and widened or narrowed the stitch width to fit. By sewing one satin-stitch row adjacent to or overlapping the next, she created a solid texture.

Technique 4: Free Motion: Free motion means that your hands instead of the feed dogs guide the forward motion on the sewing machine. Use a straight or zigzag setting for this. Read your manual to set the machine for darning. On my machine this means releasing the pressure on the presser foot and setting the stitch length to zero. The fabric is still held down to form the stitch but can slide this way or that under the foot.

If you cannot alter the pressure, use a darning or embroidery foot or spring. The embroidery foot of metal or plastic has a tiny hoop on its end to hold the fabric down, but it will ride up and down with the needle, allowing you to move the fabric during that part of the stitch. The spring does the same.

To sew, guide the fabric under the needle by moving small distances in any direction. It's easy to pull the needle off-center and break it, so move carefully. Increase the speed of the machine. The faster it goes, the more tiny stitches you'll have and the less chance of breaking the needle. It will seem strange at first to have the machine pounding away wildly while you slowly move the fabric, but soon you'll be drawing your designs in thread freely.

You can also set the machine on zigzag and the needle will swing while you guide the fabric to form the lines. This compares with shading when you draw with a colored pencil. See this effect on the kitten (Fig. 6-8) from the *Favorite Cats* project in chapter 9.

6-9. *To sew a teapot's portrait (at the left), use machine-sewn satin-stitching, zigzag-stitching, and any patterned stitch that accomplishes the effects you want.*

Technique 5: Programmed Pattern Stitches: Not only is the zigzag setting used for satin-stitch but several of the programmed pattern stitches can be altered by the machine's settings as you sew to vary the stitch. On *Family Teapot Quilt* (Fig. 6-9) I used a programmed stitch that closely matched a design on the teapot. It was manipulated several ways: by increasing and decreasing the stitch length to make the pattern longer or shorter to accommodate the bulge in the pot and by reducing the pressure on the presser foot enough to manipulate the fabric and yet the feed dogs still moved the fabric.

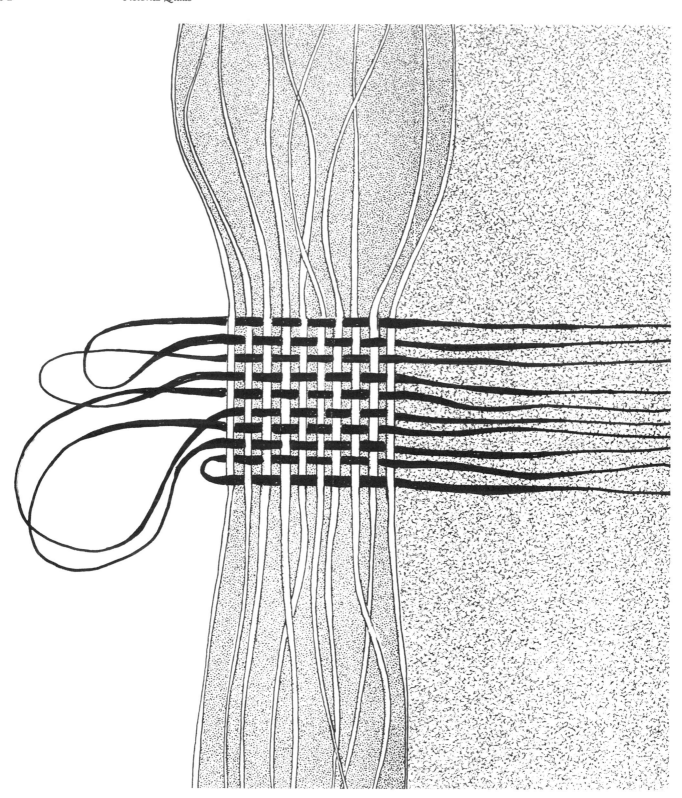

6-10. Here is the pattern for
Interweave. Scale it up to size.

PROJECT:
DRAWING BY SEWING MACHINE, *INTERWEAVE*
(Fig 6-10; and see C-23 in the color section)

Overview: In this piece, the design is sewn on canvas backing, which provides a nonpuckering surface for appliqué and machine embroidery. This center panel (called the inner panel) is stretched over a mat board square and mounted on a fabric background stretched on a frame and wired for hanging. The sewing machine becomes the artist's brush on canvas to "draw" lines of varying widths. You can follow the pattern given or meander across your canvas in any stitch and color of your choice.

Theme: The many ways that fibers can be manipulated to form fabrics or make embroideries interests me. This piece shows how the free-flowing character of yarn strands can be organized into geometric regularity as woven cloth.

Technique: Machine-embroidery.

Size: Inner panel 16-1/2" (42cm) square; mounting panel 24" (61cm) square.

MATERIALS

Inner panel: 18"(46cm) square of artist's untreated canvas or similar heavy fabric; natural-colored (oatmeal) fabric 8" x 18" (20cm x 46cm); and darker natural-colored (bran) fabric 6" x 18" (15cm x 46cm).

Background panel: 30" (76cm) square natural linen or linenlike fabric; poster board 16-1/2" (42cm) square and 24" (61cm) square; embroidery threads in white and dark brown; 1" x 2" (2cm x 4cm) framing 8' (244cm).

Tools and supplies: A ruler, a triangle, a pencil, a zigzag sewing machine, Elmer's white glue, wood glue, duct tape, hammer, nails, a staple gun and staples, and picture wire.

PROCEDURE

Scale up the pattern to full size, make your own sketch, or just start sewing and see what you turn out. It's your choice.

Prepare the Inner Panel

1 Cut out the added fabric shapes according to the diagram, leaving generous 1" (2.5cm) or more seam allowances.

2 Place the oatmeal piece on the canvas, overlapping 1" (2.5cm) at the edges and under the central added piece. Straight-stitch to baste in place.

3 On the bran-colored piece, trim 1/4" (6mm) seam allowances, hem, and pin in place over the first added piece. Straight-stitch 1/8" (3mm) from the edge to appliqué the piece in place; see chapter 7 for more details on appliqué techniques.

4 Draw the design on the fabric:

a. Use a sharp lead pencil or a white pencil (on darker fabric) to trace or draw the design on the fabric. Use drafting tools (see chapter 4) to measure and accurately draw the central grid. It measures 3-1/2" (9cm) so the grid has squares 1/3" (3mm). Measure down from the top and side seam lines 6-3/4" (17cm) to place the grid.

b. Draw the fiber lines to the edge of the canvas with white pencil or chalk on the face side or turn it over and straight-stitch a tracing line through the pattern.

Satin-Stitch the Design

1 Set your machine to satin-stitch and use a satin-stitch presser foot, as described previously. Adjust the tension control so the top thread shows on the reverse side. Practice on a scrap canvas to adjust the stitch. If this puckers, use paper backing. Set the stitch length to short (close together). If the satin-stitch does not cover, shorten the stitch length until it does. If it is too dense and piles up lengthen it.

2 Thread the top with white embroidery thread, and the bobbin with clear monofilament thread or fine sewing thread. Set the width to 1/8" (3mm) or about half of the maximum width of your zigzag. Satin-stitch downward over the hemmed edge toward the center grid, slowly increasing the width evenly as you sew. Keep your stitch line smooth and fluid by guiding the fabric with your left hand and adjusting the stitch width with your right.

3 At the grid, satin-stitch across evenly without changing the width. Resume sewing the varied line to the edge. Repeat this for every vertical white stitch line sewing over the drawn or basted lines.

4 Thread the machine with dark brown embroidery thread. Begin at the right and with a varied width until you reach the grid. Use the widest setting satin-stitch to sew straight across over the first sewn white line. To simulate weaving, on the second line stop at the edge, move the fabric ahead, and resume sewing on the other side of the stitch line still straight across. Sew across the next white line. Continue across in this manner, stitching over every other white line.

5 At the left end of the grid, follow the looped line of the pattern changing the width in an even flow as you sew. As you loop back to the grid, stitch over the first white line up to the second white line and stop. Move the fabric and begin sewing exactly at the far edge of this white line (Fig 6-11). Continue across, skipping over every other white line and satin-stitch to the edge.

6 When you've finished, clip the diagonal brown threads over the white rows in the center, leaving two small ends. Turn the piece over and pull the brown threads through to the back. Add a dot of Fray Check if this thread is slippery so it won't pull out.

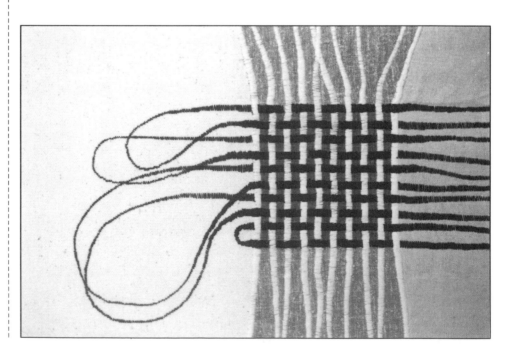

6-11. Detail of the center of Interweave

Finish the Wall Piece

1 Place the finished panel accurately on the 16-1/2" (42cm) mat board square and tape it on the back side. To do this, use duct tape along one side, pull the opposite side until it is smooth and taut, and tape that side. Pull the top smooth and tape. Pull the bottom edge smooth and tape. Make a mitered fold at the corners and tape (Fig. 6-12).

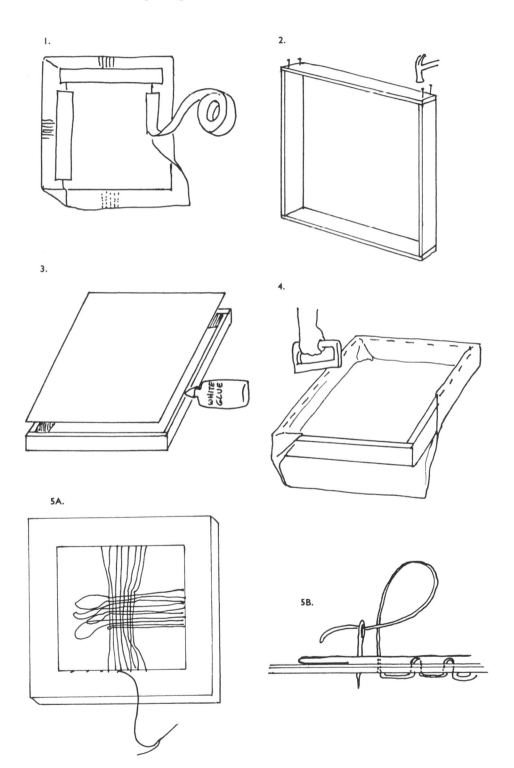

1.

2.

3.

4.

5A.

5B.

6-12. To mount machine embroideries for display, (1) stretch the piece on a 16-1/2" (42cm) square mat board and tape; (2) make a wooden 1" x 2" (2cm x 4cm) frame 24" (61cm) square; (3) glue on a 24" (61cm) square mat board; (4) stretch the linen over the frame and staple it on the back (carefully making mitered corners); and (5) sew the panel on with hidden stitches. Wire for hanging.

2 Make a 1" x 2" (2cm x 4cm) frame by cutting two 1" x 2" (2cm x 4cm) pieces 24" (61cm), and two 22-1/2" (57cm). Cut exact right-angle corners. Using 2" (5mm) finishing nails, start two nails at both ends of the 24" (61cm) pieces 3/8" (9mm) in from the end. Hammer until the nail tips show on the undersides. Spread wood glue on the end of the shorter board and align it with the longer one under the nails and even with the end of the top piece. Hammer the nails in and countersink. (Drive them below the wood surface so they don't stick up.) Repeat this for all four corners.

3 Use white glue to glue the 24" (61cm) piece of mat board to the frame top because staples will work their way out.

4 Stretch the 30" (76cm) square of fabric on this frame:

a. Staple the fabric to the frame along one edge on the back at 2" (5cm) intervals.

b. Wrap the fabric up the side, across the front, and around to the other side. Staple this fabric to the back edge in the center. Pull the fabric toward the corner and staple at 2" (5cm) intervals to the corner. Repeat in the other direction.

c. At the top edge, pull the fabric smooth and taut, but not so the grain is off on the front at the edges of the frame, and staple this edge to the frame back edge in the center. Pull the fabric toward the corner and staple as above, stopping 2" from the corner. Repeat.

d. At the corner, tuck the extra fabric under at a forty-five-degree angle so the exposed edge is straight at the corner. Pull the extra around to the back edge and staple. Do this for each corner.

5 Align the panel in the center of the frame and sew in place through the fabric and mat board with hidden stitching. Wire the back to hang.

SHAPES:
APPLIQUÉING SEVERAL WAYS

Chapter Seven

F abric pictures show shapes in different ways: to look flat or three dimensional, to be just what you see, or to represent something else. Both the subject and patterned background in the *Carousel Horse Tote Bag* project for this chapter (Fig. 7-1) are full of shapes. The cutout white pieces of fabric become a carousel horse because our minds want to make understandable pictures of what we see.

The busy background shapes are decorative, but our eyes try to make pictorial sense of these, too. We begin to see the overscaled flowers as paneling circling the carousel top. Perhaps the looping lines indicate the up-and-down swing of the horses as they spin. I liked the tension created by shapes that sorted themselves into other things. In working with shapes, sometimes you will do this consciously and sometimes intuitively, feeling your way along as you design a piece.

This piece was made by applying flat fabric shapes to a fabric background. For this we use the French word for apply, "appliqué." This sewing technique can be used to create fairly simple scenes or wonderfully elaborate ones, such as Margaret Cusack's fabric magazine illustrations. By using fabrics creatively, selecting a twill weave for a roof or a peony print for clouds, she evokes more imagery than a simple drawing would do (see C-22 and C-24 in the color section).

This chapter describes the many ways to do appliqué, each with its own advantages and accompanying problems.

HAND-SEWN APPLIQUÉ

Mary Gentry uses this ages-old technique to hand sew the figures on her wall quilt shown in chapter 1 (see Figure 1-8). Four of these characters show the effect she gets (see C-21 in the color section). She likes hand appliqué for many reasons, among them that no stitching shows and that the hemmed edges give shapes a charming rounded effect. Sewing by hand gives Mary stitch-by-stitch control of the shape and placement, making it easy for her to change her mind, add tucks and folds, or otherwise manipulate the fabric. Further, hand sewing is portable.

7-1. *The appliquéd* Carousel Horse *on a tote bag is the project for this chapter. See the instructions at the end of this chapter.*

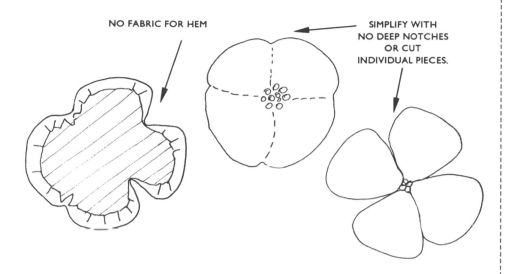

NO FABRIC FOR HEM

SIMPLIFY WITH
NO DEEP NOTCHES
OR CUT
INDIVIDUAL PIECES.

Tools and Techniques

1. Appliqué Shapes: Simplify shapes if you have a choice. Hand appliqué works best with shapes close to square or round because intricate or slender ones are too difficult to handle. Mary Gentry chooses a patterned fabric or embroidery when fine details are called for. She warns to watch for impossible shapes, such as inside corners that have no fabric for a seam allowance.

Fig. 7-2 shows how you can simplify a flower shape, for example, but don't give in all the way. You may need to push the technique to meet your needs. After all, the primary goal is create expressive imagery, and you want to maintain the integrity of each shape.

2. Appliqué Patterns: To make these, use paper, cardboard, or plastic. Template patterns with no seam allowance provide the most accurate edge line for folding a hem. If, however, you have a tendency to forget about seam allowances in the heat of placing patterns on fabric for cutting, then add narrow seam allowances all around before tracing the design. Even better, use a paper pattern to cut out with seam allowances and a template for tracing or folding the hemline.

3. Appliqué Fabrics: Firmly woven all-cotton fabrics in a tabby weave are best for hand appliqué for these reasons:

1. The tabby weave, with no threads going over more than one thread, is less apt to fray (Fig. 7-3). The twill weave, with long overshots is more apt to fray.

2. Cottons are soft and allow the needle through easily.

3. Cottons are thin and flexible for easy hemming.

4. Cottons come in a variety of plain colors and small prints that are ideal for appliqué.

Mary Gentry, in typical artist fashion, forgoes the ease of working with cotton for the rich colors and textures of a coarse wool, a lustrous panne, or a shiny metallic. To circumvent problems, she uses fairly simple shapes, makes images in sections, and holds frisky fabrics down with embroidery detailing. Some nonfraying fabric need not be hemmed, such as felt, Ultrasuede, ribbons, or leather.

7-2. *Simplify hand-hemmed appliqué shapes as much as possible. Inside corners have no seam allowance for a hem.*

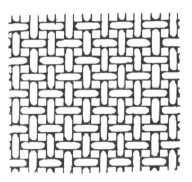

TABBY WEAVE

7-3. *Firm tabby weaves, such as quilter's cottons, are best for appliqué. Long overshot weaves, such as the twill weave, will ravel when cut.*

TWILL WEAVE

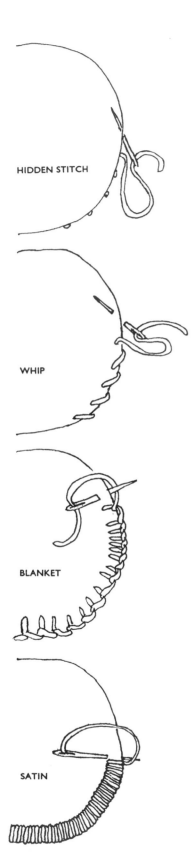

HIDDEN STITCH

WHIP

BLANKET

SATIN

7-4. The four most common hand-sewn stitches for hemming appliqué are: hidden, whip, blanket, and satin stitches.

4. Cutting Appliqué Shapes

1. If using a pattern with seam allowances added, pin it to the fabric, noting the fabric grain. Use good-quality sharp scissors to cut out the design carefully. For accuracy, add a hemming line traced around a template on the face of the fabric with removable markings.

2. If using a template alone, hold it down to trace around on the fabric's back side and use a sharp lead pencil or white pencil that will not bleed or show through. Add a seam allowance of 1/4" (6mm) or wider if the fabric might fray or is thicker than calico. Cut out the design carefully.

5. Several Ways to Hem Appliqués

1. Finger-press the hem along the contour line and pin the piece in place with dressmaker silk pins.

2. For large pieces, press the hem by steam iron and pin the pieces in place for top-stitching to hold it down.

3. If pieces must be geometrically accurate, fold and press the hem over a stiff cardboard template. Don't iron a plastic template, and watch your fingers for this step. Remove the template.

4. If an unstable fabric changes shape, the most accurate means of hemming is to baste and pick out the basting stitches later. Or use a paper template and baste the hems through the paper as in English piecing, if the sound of paper crinkle later doesn't matter; (see chapter 3).

Freezer paper works for this, too, since one side will adhere to fabric when ironed. Use a freezer paper template to anchor ironed seams in place. The paper remains inside.

5. You can use cello-tape or masking tape to tape the hems in place and then remove the tape during basting or stitching. Don't store a project long with tape on because eventually it will leave the adhesive on the fabric.

Appliqué Stitching

Use a hand-embroidery hoop to hold the fabric stable and taut while you attach pieces. These stitches are the most common (Fig. 7-4).

1. Hidden stitching   *3.* Blanket stitching
2. Whip stitching   *4.* Satin-stitching

1. To make hidden stitches, stab the needle up from the back to catch a few fibers on the edge of the added piece. Insert the needle in the background fabric a tiny stitch ahead under the piece, emerging for the next stitch to catch a few fibers at the edge of the piece. Pull the stitch firmly and repeat.

2. To whip stitch, come up within the piece, insert the needle at the edge into the background fabric, emerge within the piece ahead a stitch, pull the stitch firm, and repeat.

3. The blanket stitch, popular in the 1930s, is begun at the edge. Come up within the piece 1/16" (1.5mm) or more. Insert the needle 1/16" (1.5mm) into the piece, emerging at the edge within the loop of the stitch. Pull the stitch to form a corner-shaped stitch.

4. Satin-stitching by hand is slow and takes practice to be even, but it makes a handsome decorative edge. Sew parallel stitches over the piece edge in a solid row.

Reverse Appliqué

The San Blas people of the Panama Islands and the Hmong people of Laos use this intricate technique. They stack plain colored cotton fabrics with the main color on top and the background color beneath. Designs are cut out from the top layer and hemmed with tiny stitches. This reveals the second layer. Designs with tiny seam allowances may be cut from a lower layer as well to outline the top pieces, to add another design element, or to serve as the background. Each cut edge is carefully hemmed with hidden stitching, giving the pieces a characteristic puffy hand-sewn look that is so appealing. Often added pieces and colors are sewn or embroidered on the hemmed piece.

MACHINE APPLIQUÉ

Machine appliqué characteristics

Machine appliqué differs from hand appliqué in several ways:

- Construction methods   • Fabric hand   • Appearance   • Durability

I. Construction Methods: Construction requires that appliqué pieces be held firmly in place during stitching or they will stretch and travel on the background fabric. This happens because the machine's feed dogs move the bottom fabric and the top one is slowed by friction from the presser foot. The Pfaff sewing machine has a built-in walking foot that counteracts this. An accessory walking foot can be used if the appliqué pieces are not too intricate.

2. Fabric Hand: Because the thread is at least doubled, is tightly twisted, and is firmly sewn, machine stitching changes the fabric's hand—the way fabric feels in hand. The results may be stiffer than hand sewing, and satin-stitching may stretch or pucker the background fabric.

3. Appearance: The distinctive look of hand-hemmed appliqué held on by hidden stitching is not readily duplicated by sewing machine. However, the variety of decorative stitches for outlining offsets this; for example, you can easily blanket-stitch the edges by machine.

4. Durability: Machine-sewn appliqué is stronger than hand-sewn and has a distinctive look of its own. It is faster to do and will probably handle small pieces more readily than in hand-sewing. It allows for an added color in the outline threads, which is a way to increase the impact of the imagery.

As inventive stitchers developed new ways to appliqué, products came out to help them. This accounts for some of the growing difference between hand and machine appliqué. Brief instructions are included with the many projects in this book that involve forms of machine appliqué but information on all these techniques appears in this chapter.

Tools and Supplies

I. Patterns: Keep a good supply of pattern paper on hand because one copy of your pattern may be destroyed by the process. You will need a reverse copy of the pattern for some techniques. Tracing paper and sketching paper, which come in pads or rolls, can stand the wear and tear of the machine stitching plus you can see through it to align pattern pieces or to sew the outlines. Copy paper (cheaper than typing paper) also works well for patterns, sketching ideas, backing the fabrics, or as a pressing cloth; see chapter 1 for information on drawing patterns.

2. Fabrics: You'll be able to use a wide range of fabrics in machine appliqué. The tightly woven polycotton blends that resist hand sewing are often easier to sew by machine. Loosely woven fabric that might fray can be held down with dense stitching or with a bonded backing. Decorative fabrics, such as metallics, laces and others, can be used by adding a backing fabric for reinforcement. Tightly woven, thin tabby weave fabrics are easiest to appliqué: see chapter 9 for more on fabrics.

In placing pattern pieces, pay attention to the grain line, that is, the way the weave runs. Generally, added pieces and the background fabric should run true to the "picture frame." Off-grain applied pieces may wrinkle when hung unless sturdy backing is used. For visual reasons the grain should run in logical directions. In Margaret Cusack's *Young Woman at the Piano*, the dot-pattern wallpaper runs true, yet the moiré pattern on the piano simulating wood-graining relates more to shape (see C-23 in the color section).

Some fabrics shadow. Colors and textures show through light-colored and lightweight fabrics. To prevent this, back these fabrics with white or matching fabric. Trim overlapped fabrics carefully since rough edges may show through. Remove underfabrics that cause unsightly lumps in the appliqué; or use this characteristic to your advantage by using a bright color under a light one to shadow the top color or by letting a fluffy texture pad an appliqué.

3. Threads, needles, and sewing machines: Chapter 6 on machine embroidery describes these in detail, but to sum up:

1. Use only good-quality, nonshrink, nonfade, tightly wound threads. Fill several bobbins with clear monofilament thread so you won't need to stop to rewind. Be sure to use a strong, thin thread on the bobbin, especially for satin-stitching.

2. A zigzag sewing machine is necessary for this technique. Read chapter 6 for details on how the machine works.

3. The light box is described in chapter 4, with directions for making your own. You can hold your work up to a window for a light source from behind, but a light box is good for making patterns, tracing patterns on fabric, fitting fusibles to fabrics, aligning appliqué pieces, drawing seam lines, and more.

4. Fabric stiffeners: The biggest problem in machine appliqué is keeping the background fabric flat to avoid stretching or puckering. You need to reinforce or stabilize the fabric. There are several ways to do this, and sometimes you need to use more than one technique.

1. Hoops: For extensive machine embroidery, you want the fabric held taut and flat against the needle plate. Use plastic or wooden machine embroidery hoops, as described in chapter 6. Both are thin enough to slide under the presser foot and needle.

2. Stabilizers: More often, you will use paper or fabric backing to add stability to fabrics. Use inexpensive copy paper, typing paper—both new and used—shelf paper, tracing paper, wrapping paper, or almost any firm, thin paper. Printed newspaper may smear and coated paper may slide on the feed dogs to make guiding the fabric difficult.

Pin or stitch the paper to the background fabric on the back side, away from seam lines. Straight-stitching will perforate paper so that it can be torn off easily. Satin-stitching will do the same, except that the paper remains under the covered stitching, keeping it flat. Since other stitches may not release the paper easily, you can leave the paper in place.

Tear-away stabilizers made especially for dense machine embroideries work like paper. Liquid stabilizers can be sprayed on, let dry, and then washed out after stitching; however most wall quilts should be dusted, not washed.

The most permanent stabilizer is another layer of fabric that acts as an interfacing. This works especially well for maintaining flexibility, for backing light-colored fabrics that would shadow, and for doing away with the need for paper backing. I commonly begin an art quilt on canvas-weight backing and build up the surface with added fabrics. Even when added fabrics cover the background entirely, it's still there doing its job. The 1880s crazy quilts were made on a muslin base appliquéd with decorative fabrics overlaid with embroidery. The muslin strengthened fragile fabrics and made random "piecing" designs possible.

3. Fusibles: Heat-sensitive adhesives on the back of these products bond one fabric to another. Some interfacing fabrics come ready to bond. The good and bad of this product is that it stiffens fabric. For stability in wall-hung pieces, that's good; for clothing, that may be bad.

Adhesive webbing comes as a spidery web in rolls or strips, such as Stitch Witchery, or as webbing adhered to a release paper, such as Wonder-Under by Pellon. You can draw the appliqué design on the paper backing, trim, and press onto the fabric to make the pieces fusible. Use the light box to reverse the pattern, lay the paper-backed webbing on the pattern, and trace the design. If the pencil doesn't work, you've got the webbing side up by mistake. Turn it over and trace.

Use a covering for your ironing board, such as Teflon sheeting or grocery store parchment paper to keep your work clean and to avoid ironing adhesive on the wrong surfaces.

5. Pressing tools: Turning hems and applying adhesive webbing require an iron to apply heat. Use an iron with reliable heat controls. Consider one with a Teflon faceplate, useful for the fusing process since this can get messy. The advantage of the hand iron is that you can manipulate the piece while ironing.

A press with a face plate the same size as the padded surface, has the advantage that the fusing pieces do not move. Keep the face plates scrupulously clean on both or you will press smears and stains onto your work. Use parchment paper under and/or over it during the fusing process since the webbing will not adhere to it. Use an iron cleaner like Dritz Iron-off to clean the plate. Don't scrape or sandpaper the faceplate or you'll roughen it up.

Machine Surface Stitching

Outline stitching, particularly satin-stitching, does three important things: it holds the appliqué piece securely to the background fabric; it covers the raw edges of the fabric neatly; and it provides a chance for artistic embellishment. Read chapter 6 on machine embroidery for stitch information (Fig. 7-5).

7-5. The peony on his relative's block from David and Tori Goodrich's wedding quilt shows one of the many ways to machine appliqué. Additional satin-stitching highlights the petals.

1. Stitch Width: The fabric type and the kind of wear expected influence the width of satin-stitch needed to hold the piece securely. Loosely woven fabrics, such as twill or burlap weaves, will need a wide stitch. A child's quilt will need a very wide stitch indeed, as appliquéd pieces are not as flexible as surrounding fabric and the edges pull out with wear.

2. Stitch Coverage: Stitch length controls the density of satin-stitching. The softness of the embroidery thread affects coverage. A lace or similar irregular weave may need to be satin-stitched with a plastic bag overlay to hold loose ends down neatly. A fragile fabric that will fray, such as a metallic, may need a fused backing, as well as a wide stitch for a neat edge.

3. Colors: Satin-stitching the edge and adding machine embroidery articulate the imagery. On David and Tori Goodrich's wedding quilt (see Fig. 7-5), the peony was enlivened with a darker shade of pink. A few petals were highlighted with light pink stitching, and the center stamens glow in yellow stitching. The leaves looked richer with a dark green edging.

Plan the outline colors when you make the pattern. Sometimes a zany color combination is just right, such as an orange thread on purple or pink on green. Adding colored threads can improve an off-color. When a piece is too similar to the background, outlining with a darker or brighter thread will articulate it. If you don't want the outline to show, match the thread to the appliqué piece.

The storybook quilt block (Fig. 7-6) by Lois Goodrich shows this even in black and white. The white duck needs a white outline on a dark background. The light yellow ducklings were enlivened with a gold outline.

4. Stitching: Set the sewing machine tension control looser so the top thread shows on the back, and adjust the stitch width and length until the coverage is the way you want it. Use stabilizing paper on the back. Plan the stitch lines so the main outline comes last to overlap any stitch lines it crosses. On the peony, the pink flower outline covers the ends of the green leaf outline. When you've finished, pull the thread ends to the back. Secure them with Fray Check or knot them.

5. Reverse Stitching: To add heavy threads, sew surface details from the underside. Use embroidery thread on the bobbin and clear or matching sewing thread on the top. Set the top thread tension loose enough to loop around the bobbin thread but not so loose that it loops. Sew as usual or free-sew the design on a darn setting.

7-6. Lois Goodrich appliqués quilts for all occasions. This detail from a storybook quilt made for Michael Guy Goodrich's arrival shows the fabled ugly duckling.

Techniques for Machine Appliqué

These techniques are similar yet each has a special feature. For example, use machine hemming for crazy quilts; use sewing through the pattern for accuracy; use sewing from the back for placement; use stacked appliqué for efficiency; use reverse appliqué for intricacy; and use fusing for smoothness.

1. Machine-hemmed appliqué
2. Appliqué through the pattern
3. Appliqué from the back
4. Stacked appliqué
5 Reverse appliqué
6. Fused appliqué

1. Machine-Hemmed Appliqué: To machine hem, proceed as in hand appliqué; make the patterns, cut out the pieces, and press or baste the hems. Pin or clear tape the pieces in place on the background fabric and appliqué by top-stitching along the edge. Some shapes and fabrics will work better than others for this, such as fabrics folded on grain or simple shapes.

Use any stitch that gives the effect you want: a straight stitch; a basting stitch covered by satin-stitching; a blind hem stitch like the blanket stitch to give a hand-sewn texture to the edge; a feather stitch to give the embroidered look of a crazy quilt; or a scallop stitch to look like a wrapped teapot handle as I did in the upper left on the *Family Teapot Quilt* (see Fig. 2-1 in chapter 2). Try every stitch, including those little ducks and dogs some machines include.

If the appliqué piece moves or puckers when you attempt to sew it, lay a clear plastic bag or sheer tracing paper over it, pin this in place, and sew the pieces down through the plastic or paper. The bag or paper will tear off. Remains of the plastic will show through an open zigzag or pattern stitch, so use a straight stitch or solid satin-stitch to cover.

2. Appliqué Through the Pattern: Once you discover you can sew through paper, the quilting world opens up. You can draw a pattern, lay it on the fabrics, and sew them in place through the pattern. The paper serves three purposes: as a pattern; to hold the added pieces in place; and to stabilize the fabric layers for stitching. Appliqué through the pattern can be done three ways: from the back, stacked, and in reverse, as described below.

To begin, make a pattern. Sketch something from your garden, trace an image from a book, or borrow an image from some other source that can be reduced to flat colors, such as the peony (see Fig. 7-5).

Lay tracing paper over your sketch and trace the flat color areas. As an example, see the *Little Red Riding Hood* project in chapter 5. If some areas don't make sense, alter the pattern. Where two sets of leaves overlap, choose different colors to show this. Simplify the pattern as much as possible yet maintain the integrity of the original. The leaf shapes and the notch in the petal make the peony unmistakable.

Once you've done these steps, proceed with one of the next three techniques.

3. Appliqué from the Back: Trace two copies of your pattern, one in reverse. Pin the reversed copy on the back of the background fabric (Fig. 7-7). Use the other to cut up for pattern pieces, adding wide seam allowances. You can either sew all the outlines through the pattern, for easier aligning of appliqué pieces or, if this is too time consuming, use a light box to align pieces on the top and place pins out of the seam lines.

Mary Gentry sketches her imagery in reverse directly on Thermo-lam, a fluffy interfacing that is heavy enough to withstand the puckering of zigzag stitching. Working from the back she sews the design with a freewheeling line. "I like this technique," Mary says, "because you can see where you've sewn." She often designs her pieces as she goes, working only generally from a sketch instead of a pattern.

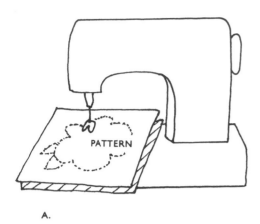

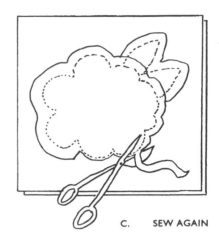

A.

B. PLACE APPLIQUÉ PIECES

C.   SEW AGAIN

7-7. For easy appliqué, pin the pattern (reversed) to the fabric back and sew through the lines for placement of appliqué pieces on the front. Sew again to anchor the pieces and then trim away seam allowances.

To align appliqué pieces, you don't need a light box if you stitched through the pattern or drawn lines. Use the stitch lines on the front for positioning and pin or tape the appliqué piece in place. It will cover the lines, so flip it over and resew the lines to anchor the piece. Trim away the excess fabric. Place the next piece and repeat the process. You will be able to see by the stitch lines where one piece overlaps another. Complete the piece by satin-stitching over the raw edges.

4. Stacked Appliqué: This technique is a one-step version of sewing through the pattern. The pattern paper or a copy of it with the fabrics stacked behind it acts as the stitching guide. All excess fabric is trimmed off after stitching. The stacking technique is more accurate than iron-on fusibles and keeps a soft hand to the fabric. It works well for two or three colors but gets complicated with several layers.

1. To assemble the stack, cut out pattern shapes in fabric bigger than the final shape. See the peony diagram (see Fig. 7-7) as an example to see how this works. Later, the excess gets trimmed off.

2. Tape the pattern face side down on the light box or window and put the largest fabric piece face down on the pattern and adjust it so it covers the lines visible through the pattern. If this is a light color, check for shadowing and use a backing fabric, if needed. Tape or pin it to the paper outside all the stitch lines. Add the next color, the green pin-dot leaf fabric, adjusted to its area and tape in place. Add all fabrics until the stack is complete.

Note: Tape is safer than pins, which might be hidden in the stack or which might jam the sewing machine.

3. Turn the stack over, paper side up. To baste, set your sewing machine to a short, narrow zigzag stitch. Use a clear thread or a bland color. It will be covered and won't show. Stitch all the lines of the pattern through the paper.

4. Tear the pattern away from the stitch lines. Consult your tracing with colors marked and trim the excess fabric outside the zigzag stitching to less than 1/8" (3mm) using appliqué or sharp embroidery scissors. Where one piece overlaps another, as the pink peony overlaps the green leaves, trim all excess pink fabric and pull the pink fibers out of the leaf stitch line. Trim the leaves. Outline-stitch the appliqué to finish.

5. *Reverse Appliqué:* This technique works just like stacked appliqué except you will use the overlaps as the San Blas people do on their molas. An example of this technique is the dart board on the *Game Quilt* (See Fig. 7-8), the project for chapter 4.

1. Make a copy of your pattern in reverse if you plan to sew from the back. Use your pattern or planning sketch to refer to when trimming seam allowances later.

2. Cut out all the added colors the full size of the total pattern. Don't use more than three colors, as it gets too thick. Make a layered stack in this order: stabilizer if needed; background fabric; the third least used color; the second color; and the most-used color on top. Pin the layers together outside the stitch lines. Pin the pattern to the top or the reversed pattern to the back.

3. Sew all the lines of the pattern design from the back or front through the pattern, as above, using a narrow zigzag stitch. Tear off the pattern pieces.

4. Consult your pattern to locate a part of the design where the second color will show. Pinch up the fabric to separate it from the background and snip with scissors to make an opening. Trim away the top color fabric very close to the stitch line to expose the second color. Do this everywhere the second color appears (Fig. 7-9).

5. For the third color, trim away the first color and the second color everywhere the third color should appear.

6. Satin-stitch over the zigzag stitching and trimmed edges to finish the piece.

6. *Fused Appliqué:* Details for this come in the project for the *Carousel Horse Tote Bag.* Surface stitching to finish the appliqué is covered first.

7-8. The dart board target from the Game Quilt (see Fig. 4-1 and C-12 in the color section), with its intricate pieces, is reverse appliquéd by sewing machine, a different technique than hand-sewn reverse appliqué.

7-9. In machine-sewn reverse appliqué, sew the design through fabric layers and then carefully clip away to the desired fabric color layer.

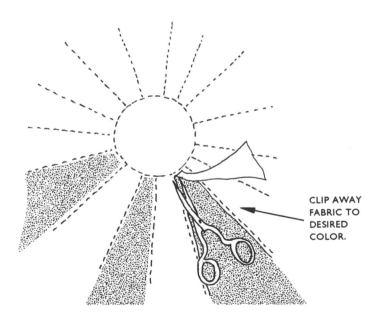

CLIP AWAY FABRIC TO DESIRED COLOR.

7-10. The Carousel Horse Tote Bag *pattern for the design panel is given in reverse.*

PROJECT:
FUSING FABRICS, *CAROUSEL HORSE TOTE BAG*
(Fig. 7-10; and see C-24 in the color section)

Overview: An appliquéd design panel of manageable size is sewn onto a tote bag before assembly. The inventive bag construction—adapted from a Monique bag whose clever designer is unknown—is easy to assemble, and serves as a tote or a backpack.

Theme: This tote bag is for my sister, Lois Goodrich, who has loved merry-go-rounds ever since our brother, Bob, and other neighborhood kids got the merry-go-round started by themselves one rainy Fourth of July. We rode and rode until we were dizzy . . . and the owners returned.

Techniques: (1) Fused fabric appliqué; and (2) satin-stitched outlines as accent colors and anchoring threads.

Size: Bag 16" x 21" (40cm x 53cm) plus strap; design panel 9-1/2" x 12" (24cm x 30cm).

MATERIALS

1-1/3 yards (114cm) of blue denim.

Patterned background fabric: 9-1/2" x 12" (24cm x 30cm).

Horse: White broadcloth 7" x 10" (18cm x 25cm), gray 3" x 4" (8cm x 10cm).

Saddle: Tan broadcloth 4" x 4" (10cm x 10cm).

Blanket: Metallic brocade 3" x 6" (8cm x 15cm).

Armor: Metallic silver 3" x 3" (8cm x 8cm).

Note: Use the colors suggested or assemble a collection of fabrics that express the feeling you want.

Zipper: 16" (40cm).

Threads: Matching blue sewing thread; white, pink, rust, ecru, gold, and black embroidery threads.

Tools: A sewing machine, scissors, pins, paper-backed fusible webbing (such as Wonder-Under), paper, parchment paper, or Teflon sheeting.

A. TRACE ON FUSIBLE

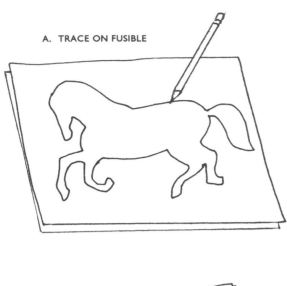

B. IRON ON FABRIC

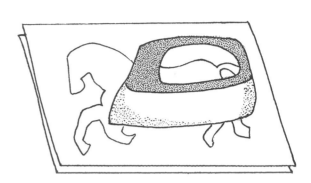

C.   TRIM AWAY EXTRA

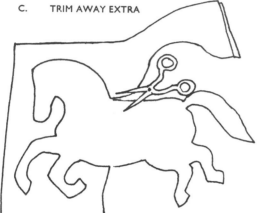

D.   IRON ON BACKGROUND.

7-11. Trace the appliqué pieces on paper-backed fusible webbing, iron this on the fabric, trim the edges, remove the paper, and then fuse the piece to the bag.

PROCEDURE

To Make the Panel, Use the Pattern Given or Make Your Own.

Make a full-sized pattern in reverse. You won't need a paper pattern for the bag.

Cut Out All the Fabric and Pattern Pieces

For the tote bag cut two pieces 17-1/2" x 22-1/2" (44cm x 57cm) and one strip 48" x 5" (122cm x 13cm); central design panel: 10-1/2" x 13" (27cm x 33cm); cut according to the printed fabric design pattern.

To Make the Central Design Panel (Fig. 7-11)

1 Trace the background panel on the paper side of fusible webbing. Cut out with 1/4" (6mm) seam allowances. Drop all small trimmings in a wastebasket to avoid ironing them on unintentionally.

2 Lay the background piece face down on paper to protect the ironing board surface. Position the webbing paper on the back and iron the webbing paper on, using the cotton heat setting for three seconds or until the webbing adheres. The color of the paper darkens slightly when this happens.

3 Trim the paper and fabric on the drawn outline. When you are ready to mount the fabric on the denim, peel off the paper backing. Position the fused panel on the denim 3-3/4" (9.5cm) up from the bottom edge and centered in from the sides about 4-3/4" (12cm).

Note: This double layer does away with the need for stabilizing paper on the back.

4 On the fusible webbing paper, trace a pattern of the horse, including the whole shape except for the gray legs. Trace webbing paper patterns for the gray legs, the saddle, the blanket, and the neck armor. Leave small seam allowances and trim them apart.

5 Position the webbing pattern for the horse on the back of the white fabric. Cover with parchment paper and iron to fuse it on. The paper protects your iron faceplate from getting sticky and ruining your work. White fabrics shadows so use a double layer of white, bonding both layers. Trim the horse on the lines. Repeat for all added pieces.

6 Position the horse and iron it onto the background. Add the gray legs, the saddle blanket, the saddle, and the mane cover and fuse all.

Note: When using Wonder-Under, iron it on metallics from the back since this fabric will be damaged by heat. A fusible called HeatnBond is available that adheres at a lower temperature.

7 Stabilize the background fabric with added paper, if needed.

8 Satin-stitch embroider around the appliqué pieces in this order: use white around the horse including his ear; pink around the horse blanket, neck trim, and panel edges; rust around the saddle and to make the hoofs; ecru to accent the saddle; gold for the silver armour; and black for head detailing. Sign your name in free-motion stitching if you wish.

Assemble the Bag

1 Center and sew the zipper to the top edge of the denim bag side. To do this, align the zipper face-to-face with the bag fabric edge. Using a wide long zigzag, sew along this edge. Fold the bag denim back from the zipper and top-stitch along the edge of the zipper. Align the opposite side and sew the zipper to it in the same manner. Align and sew the rest of the seam on each side (Fig. 7-12).

7-12. To assemble the tote bag, sew the zipper to each bag side at the top edge. Seam remaining edges to join the halves.

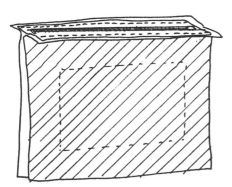

A. SEW ZIPPER TO BAG HALVES ON BACK SIDE.

B. TOP-STITCH ZIPPER ON FRONT SIDE.

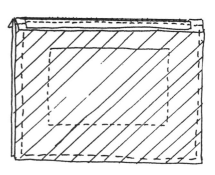

C. OPEN ZIPPER— SEAM REMAINING EDGES.

2 Open the zipper. Lay the bag sides face-to-face and sew all around the edges with a 5/8" (15mm) seam allowance. Leave it wrong side out.

3 To make the strap, fold the denim strip lengthwise down the center and press. Fold the edges in so the finished piece is 1-1/4" (3cm) wide and press. On the machine, zigzag (or use some other decorative stitch) along both sides for the entire length.

4 At one lower corner, fold the bag to match the side and bottom seams (Fig. 7-13). Clip a 1/2" (13mm) triangle off the corner tip. From inside the bag, push the strap into this slot. Align the raw end of the strap with the trimmed tip and sew across two or three times. Make sure the strap is not twisted and then do the same for the opposite lower corner.

5 Turn the bag right side out. Fold the base of the strap up 2" (5cm) on the bag and align the strap with the side seam (Fig. 7-14). Fold the top corner flat, aligning the seams to make a triangle. Pin the triangle to the strap up 12" (30.5cm) from the base (or as needed) and top stitch in place. Repeat for the other side.

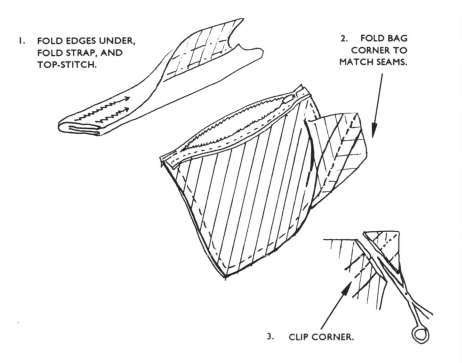

1. FOLD EDGES UNDER, FOLD STRAP, AND TOP-STITCH.

2. FOLD BAG CORNER TO MATCH SEAMS.

3. CLIP CORNER.

4. INSERT STRAP. SEW.

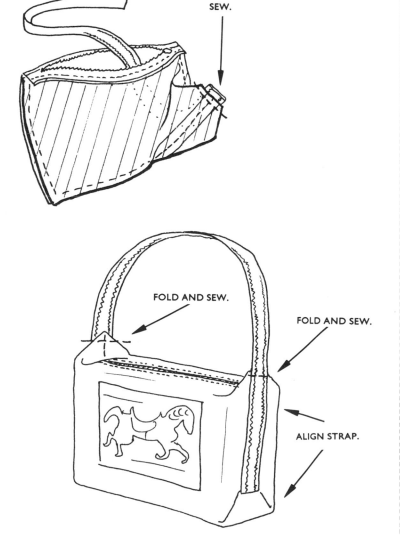

FOLD AND SEW.

FOLD AND SEW.

ALIGN STRAP.

7-13. To attach the strap, fold the bag to match the corner seams. Clip 1/2" (13mm) off the corner tip. From inside, insert the strap into this slot. Align the raw edges and sew across two or three times. Align the strap and repeat for the opposite lower corner.

7-14. Turn the bag right side out and align the strap with the side seam. Fold the top corner flat, aligning the seams, and top stitch in place. Repeat for the other side.

8-1. *Crayon transfer is an easy way to apply color to fabric. To make one like Hattie's Quilt, 38-1/2" x 50-1/2" (98cm x 128cm), find fabric crayons at the art store and polished cotton at the fabric store.*

COLORS: BEGUILING THE EYE

Chapter Eight

Color is ephemeral. It changes in sunlight and in shadow; it alters in combination with other colors; and it registers differently in people's eyes. You cannot tell color by touch but you can feel it emotionally. Color makes a black-and-white scene come to life.

We each have a built-in color sense related to the experiences in our lives and how we perceive color. This affects how we use color to express what we feel. It's a powerful tool. Compare the black-and-white photos showing how to make *Little Red Riding Hood* (see Fig. 5-1) in chapter 5, with the color reproduction of it in the color section (C-17). There's no way to describe the color of the hood to people who haven't experienced red with their own eyes.

This chapter tells the bare basics about color, about ways to combine colors, and about several ways to apply colors to fabrics. It concludes with an easy project for applying color, *Hattie's Quilt* (Fig. 8-1). Fig. 8-2 shows six-year-old Hattie Stroud, using crayon transfer colors to make her quilt blocks for this project. Techniques include direct and transfer coloring, and assembly of the patches by a continuous-string.

8-2. *Hattie Stroud is coloring designs on white typing paper to be ironed onto her quilt blocks. She drew some designs directly on the fabric blocks with fabric pastel.*

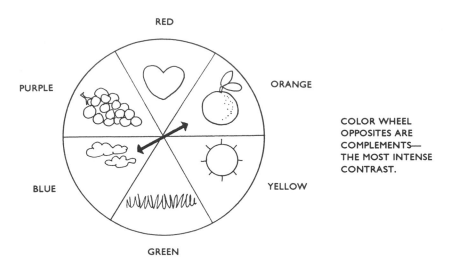

COLOR WHEEL
OPPOSITES ARE
COMPLEMENTS—
THE MOST INTENSE
CONTRAST.

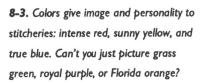

8-3. Colors give image and personality to stitcheries: intense red, sunny yellow, and true blue. Can't you just picture grass green, royal purple, or Florida orange?

COLOR: A POWERFUL TOOL

Color Basics

• Hue is the name of the color, red, yellow, blue, orange, green, and purple.

• Value is the light or darkness of a color, from black to white, maroon to pink, or navy to light blue.

• Chroma is the intensity of a color, from kelly green to muted gray-green, or from sun yellow to taupe.

A color scheme can be based on any one of these; for example, a range of different hues, of light to dark values, or of bright to muted intensities. Use a light, a bright, and a dark color, one rule says, and you will probably achieve an harmonious color scheme, such as pink (light), green (intense), and brown (dark and muted). Light colors float; reds advance; dark colors are heavy. The main thing to remember is that colors have many properties for you to use:

• Red, yellow, and blue are the three primary hues because they cannot be mixed from other colors.

• Orange, green, and purple are secondaries because they are each mixed with two primaries: red and yellow make orange, yellow and blue make green, and red and blue make purple.

• These six bright colors are arranged in a circle on a color wheel so you can easily see the opposite/complementary color of each.

• Mix a primary and a secondary (next to each other on the wheel) to get an intense tertiary (third) color, such as yellow and green to make lime. Neighboring colors like these are called analogous colors (Fig. 8-3).

The above colors are all intense, pure chroma. To see how intense, put two complementary colors (exactly opposite on the color wheel) side by side and watch the effect jiggle your eyes. Op (as in optical art) artists of the 1970s used this phenomenon to create dynamic optical effects. All painters learn to use this effect to some degree, most more subtly by diminishing the intensity to a more muted shade.

As a flat disk, the color wheel doesn't have a place for all those hundreds of other wonderful shades. There is another system for this. Assume the wheel is a book standing on end with the pages fanned, and each page is a hue, red, red-orange, orange, and so on. Each hue page contains a grid of a hundred shades of color varied in value and intensity (Fig. 8-4). Add black to darken the hue and white to lighten it (or clear to dilute it, depending on the type of paint or dye). Mix a hue with its opposite complement to mute it toward gray. Mix tones of two hues and turn to the hue page between them to find the color. In this manner, you could mix any color imaginable.

Using Color

How does knowing color theory help? Think of colors as personalities. Neighbors might get along better than those wild characters from across town, and yet a little excitement from across town might be just what the gathering needs. Try different color personalities together:

1. Combine the primary colors red, yellow, blue, orange, green, and purple for excitement. Janet Page-Kessler does this in *After the Fall* (see C-25 in the color section). Her agitated shapes augment the colors. She "holds the colors down" with gray and black accents.

2. Use muted shades to calm the scene. Margaret Cusack lightens colors to make them gentle in a serene horizontal setting (see C-26 in the color section).

3. Contrast colors for emphasis by using complementary colors, by countering light colors with dark, or by contrasting muted colors with bright. Look in the color sections for examples of this.

4. Relate colors for harmony. In the color section each scene has a color personality, whether sweet, heavy, tough, or lively.

Leslie Masters Villani, a noted Michigan painting teacher, says that her students tend to divide into two categories: Some are very cautious, want to know the rules for achieving harmony, and never break them; others want to throw everything into every painting. She encourages people to find out which type they are so the timid ones can aim for a livelier spark and the wild ones can learn some control. The goal for each is to learn to balance similarities and differences. Study the pieces in the color section and figure out what the artist's color theme or idea is.

The six basic colors in brightest intensity will always look like a crowd shouting as they vie equally for attention. Few artists use this combination, since it's hard to calm down. B. J. Adams is one who can. She likes using the primaries but in wonderfully sophisticated ways. In the *Bungy Attitude* detail in the color section (see C-20 in the color section), she uses intense colors to express an intense experience. B. J. increases the vibrating effect by stepping the colors from red to pink to mauve to purple in jiggly lines.

In *Mixed Metaphor* (see C-27 in the color section) she uses a similar delicious color range but lightens the value of all the colors to look like sherbet ice cream. You begin to notice the imagery rather than dwell on the excitement of the color—but you still revel in her colors.

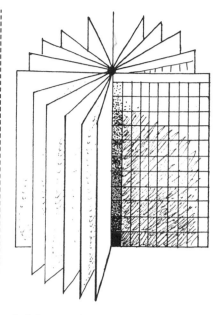

8-4. Imagine the color wheel as a book that is standing on end with pages and pages of hues, each page a single color, ranging from bright to muted and light to dark tones.

Choosing Colors

1. Try Fabrics Together: Think of color as emotion. As you put various fabrics together, keep asking yourself what you feel. Is this the emotional impact you want the piece to have? If it doesn't feel right, keep subtracting or adding colors until it does. What quilter hasn't spent hours in the fabric store heaping bolts of fabric together to get just the right combination? Try everything, whether you think it will go or not. You might discover something wonderful. Make your pictorial quilt in colors you love, because it is going to take a while and will last forever, or vice versa.

2. Consult Nature: Examine flowers closely or watch the countryside while driving to see how colors interact. A gray-green leaf may have red veins; a common dove glows with soft iridescent colors; and a stormy sky can look heavier than silvery wind-tossed leaves.

3. Read Magazines: Read home and fashion magazines to see what colors are in and how designers have combined them. You might hate a new combination in April but love it by September.

4. Study Other Artists: Study color combinations in paintings to see how artists get their effects and try ones that delight you in your own work. For fierce or angry effects, try colors that stir you to these emotions.

5. Test Color Combinations: Make a sketch of your idea and make several photocopies of it. Use children's markers, Prismacolor pencils, colored paper cutouts, or other ways of applying color to test different color combinations on your design. Tape them up, look at them for a while, and then try some more.

Fabric Colors

Fabric characteristics affect their colors.

1. Texture: Imagine a pink broadcloth. With its flat, tight weave, the color shows more than the texture. It's a flat pink. The pile weave of a pink velveteen catches shadows and highlights, making a rich changeable pink. The shiny fibers and overshot weave of satin make a lustrous pink.

2. Weight: Woolly fabrics visually outweigh thin cottons. Fiber pieces made totally from the same kind of fabric have consistency. Artists and designers learn by practice which materials go together and then delight in marrying strange ones for effect.

3. Thickness: Thin fabrics shadow, which means showing the undercolor or texture through them. Line light fabrics to prevent this, and fold seam allowances toward darker colors. You can use this to your advantage. Put yellow under white to warm it, or blue under it for coolness. Shadow embroidery does this.

4. Relationships: Rule number one with color is: Change one color and you change them all. Colors are always relative to each other. Sky blue is darker than a white cloud, lighter than the green grass. Run some black clouds through and the grass glows light and bright in a patch of sun.

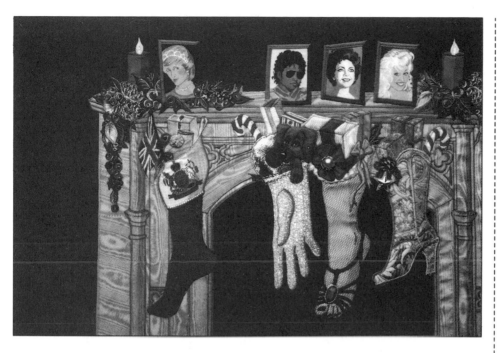

8-5. Margaret Cusack uses fabric colors and colorful textures in her Celebrity Stockings *fabric collage.*

Ways to Apply Color

Ideally, you could dash off to the fabric store and get just the range of colors you want for a project. Just as often, you need a fabric color you can't find. This has led many fabric artists to apply their own color by age-old and new techniques. This trend is not limited to artists. Walk through your crafts store to see tubes, jars, and squeeze bottles of various kinds of paint that anybody can use.

At best, color added to fabric becomes permanent, does not "crock," meaning rub off or wash out, is easy and safe to apply, and does not change the hand or feel of the fabric. Manufacturers of paints, dyes, and other materials have not come up with one that does it all. Following are some of the ways people use these supplies and the effects they achieve.

1. Use Fabrics as They Come: Nancy Jane Collins, a contemporary Grandma Moses in style (see Fig. 1-7 in chapter 1), limits herself to plain cotton and calico prints in muted colors, which she cuts to shape and hand-hems in place. Margaret Cusack also uses available colors, but in a wider variety of fabrics. In *Celebrity Stockings* (Fig. 8-5) she uses moiré for the fireplace, net for the hose, brocade for the cowboy boots, metallic weave for the glove, fur for the dog, and a variety of appliquéd threads to complete the scene. Machine appliqué lends itself to multiple color areas enhanced with threads and added trim.

To work this way, build a collection to have on hand when inspiration hits. Search the fabric stores for colors you like or need. Sometimes buy on speculation—you know you'll use it sometime. Since seasonal fabrics and color styles change, haunt the secondhand stores and rummage sales for interesting fabrics from past eras. Save clothing you've liked and cut it up for fabrics. Use quilting catalogues for ordering fabrics especially selected for quilters (see "Sources") such as sky prints, stone patterns, or tiny flowers. Develop a storage system for easy access to your trove.

2. Dyes: Dyeing fabric keeps the same hand or flexibility because the color becomes part of the fiber. This means the dye has to penetrate the fiber; for permanence, it must bond with it. Dyes must be "set" either with heat or by a chemical reaction. This is why you iron, steam, add vinegar, or other chemicals to various dyes to set them. Most dyes work best with natural fibers: cotton, silk, linen and wool. Others have been developed for synthetic fibers.

Silk is a mainstay fabric for fiber artists because of the brilliant way it accepts dyes. Fiber-reactive dyes that achieve such sensuous colors must be steam-heat set for permanence. Batik resist, that keeps the dye from penetrating certain areas of the fabric, is one method for creating imagery. The resistance can come from hot wax, wax crayons, squeeze-on paint, fabric folds or knots, pressure, or other methods. To achieve complex effects you can dye fabric one color and then over-dye it with another, and then yet another.

Clearly you must know color mixing to predict what will result. For example, if you paint on a wax resist, dye a silk fabric red, and iron the wax out you get a red and white design. Next put wax over white formerly waxed areas that you want to keep white, and over red-dyed areas where you want red. Dye the piece green. The result will be white, red, and green images on a gray-brown background. (Mixed complements mute colors: green plus red equals gray-brown.)

Mary Gentry used Procion dyes thickened to paint consistency, brushing on the colors straight or diluted to achieve her results, as in her garden of color (see C-28 in the color section).

The Malaysian batik is done in a similar manner (Fig. 8-6). The fabric is tied between posts like a tightly stretched hammock. The artist uses a tjanting, a little metal cup with a spout, to draw designs in hot wax on the fabric. The wax outlines each area to keep colors from mixing as the dye color is painted on all at once. At times the color gets past the wax fence and runs into the adjacent color, and sometimes dye colors are purposely added so they will mix on the fabric. Some traditional batik designs are block printed on the fabric in wax. By wadding the piece into the dye bath the characteristic crackle appears where the wax breaks.

Those wild T-shirts you see are tie-dyed with strings or knots to resist the dye (Fig. 8-7). For circle shapes, poke up a piece and begin wrapping it with string. Dip in a dye bath, rinse out the extra color and set the color. Retie the area with

8-6. The white lines show where trailed wax resisted dye-painted colors on this Malaysian batik skirt detail.

TIE-DYE

A. TIE FABRIC
WITH STRING.

DIP OR BOIL IN
DYE BATH.

B. DIP IN DYE BATH.

C. FOLD AND CLAMP
FABRIC THEN DYE
FOR RESIST DESIGNS.

string, exposing different areas to dye and then redye. You need not dip dye; you can paint the dye on. To learn more about the many ways to dye fabrics, read books or specific dye instructions on the products.

3. Bleaching fabrics: A midway step, to dye or not to dye, is to bleach color out of dyed fabrics. Start with that collection of fabrics you've assembled or new fabric store selections, plain or printed. Begin with all-cotton fabrics since you will get enough surprises without coping with synthetic fabrics. Work in a ventilated space. Dip or paint the bleach on full strength or diluted, wait for the color you want (or that you get), and immediately soak it in soapy water to wash out the bleach. Move fast because you can weaken the fabric beyond use after more than a minute in full-strength bleach. The surprise comes when black fabric may bleach out to red or blue or something else. This depends on the base color of the fabric or on the relative strength of the dye colors. This technique provides shaded effects that aren't possible with appliqué alone.

4. Paints: Artist acrylic paints provide several advantages: the wonderful range of color pigments available; the ease of use since they are water soluble; and the permanence of the result. Colors can be brushed on, dipped in a wash, stippled through stencils, block printed, or other. The disadvantage is the stiffening of the fabric where the pigment is applied. If the colors are applied in a thin coating, the piece can be hand- or machine-quilted.

5. Printing: Marilyn Price used the screen-printing process for her imagery, a process described in chapter 5. The advantages of this technique are several: The image is crisp-edged; more than one copy can be made from the original screen; and the colors can be printed serially or mixed in the screen for a graded effect. Best of all, if screen-printing dye is used, the fabric will have the same hand as a commercially dyed piece and can be hand- or machine-sewn easily. Textile paint colors can be used but the fabric will be stiffer from the pigment lodged in the fibers.

6. Trying everything: Erma Martin Yost (see C-1 in the color section), noted for her beautiful colors, does not limit herself to one method of applying color. Coming from a background of Mennonite quilters, she reinterprets and combines quilt designs with other media: "The fabrics I use are hand-painted or hand-printed by myself. The printing processes are photographic: cyanotype, Kwik-

8-7. Tie-dye, an easy way to apply color to fabric, can be done several ways: string-tied and dipped; painted or dipped; and folded and clamped.

print, Inkodye, and Xerox transfers. To create the image, I use Kodalith negatives, actual objects (solar grams), or drawings on tracing paper. For the hand-painted fabric, I use acrylic and metallic paints, iridescent pigments, fabric pastels, and markers. All of these fabrics are cut up and machine embroidery is added before and after reassembly."

Margaret Cusack is another who tries everything. She often uses plain or printed color fabrics to accomplish her effects, but this does not always provide the detailing she wants: "Since my work is used as illustration and is photographed, the ways I choose to apply color need not be permanent. Sometimes I use a marker to highlight areas or fabric paint or dyes." In *Thai Airlines* (see C-29 in the color section) she used a Rit dye bath to make the sky, dipping the fabric to get a graded color.

7. *Fabric Crayons and Pastels:* Fabric crayons and fabric pastels apply color easily to fabric. The fabric crayons are made of colored pigment combined with wax. Drawings are first made on paper. When heat is applied, the wax melts into the fabric and binds the color there. The crayon drawings may look dull on paper but the color intensifies and blends under heat, depending on the base fabric. Fabric pastels, similar to fabric crayons, are drawn directly on the fabric. These colors are more intense but the thicker pastel is too wide and soft to make detailed drawings without extreme care. Both can be washed when finished and still retain good color.

8-8. The author's Self Portrait drawings: (top) a marker-drawn sketch as a guide for her view of herself; and (bottom) sewing a quilt using fabric pastels (at right) on fabric taped to the table.

In *Self Portrait* (Fig. 8-8) I used fabric pastels directly on warm white polished-cotton fabric. The ecru fabric color of the border muted the pastel colors and pulled them together. "What's going on here?" people ask at first sight of this piece, but as stitchers you will recognize that it's what you see when sewing (see chapter 3 on perspective). The photo shows my original rough sketch at the top, the fabric pastel drawing taped down around the edges to keep it smooth, and the supplies on the right, including other stuff sitting around on my worktable. The piece was designed to be hand-quilted so the puffiness would contribute to the design.

Using the pastels directly on fabric is like drawing on rough paper. Bits of color adhere to the high points so you can't get a smooth wash effect. In addition, a blot of color appears at the end of a stroke if you reverse. This means you need to stroke and lift. Colors are limited, but by coloring one over another and another, you can get some lively mixes. Working with the crayon transfers gives smoother effects because the paper is smoother. Try mixing the techniques (Fig. 8-9).

Both crayons and pastels are heat-set and give off hydrocarbon fumes, so work in a ventilated room. It takes a hot iron to set them so supervise children or do the pressing for them. Further instructions for direct pastel drawing and fabric transfer crayons follow in the project.

8-9. Try various kinds of strokes to see how a transfer-crayon or fabric pastel drawing works best on smooth paper and textured fabric.

PATTERN AND
DIAGRAM FOR
ASSEMBLY

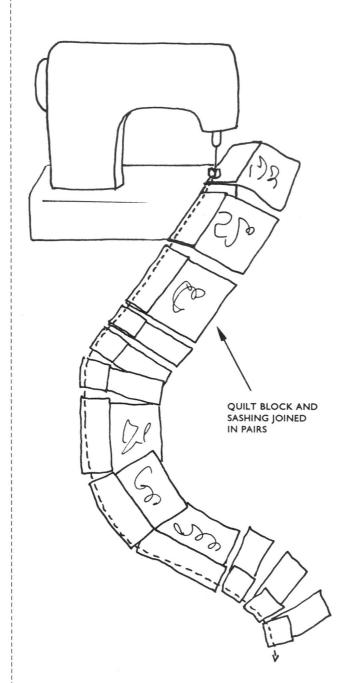

QUILT BLOCK AND
SASHING JOINED
IN PAIRS

8-10. *To assemble the quilt face in this standard grid and sashing pattern, cut the pieces accurately and machine-seam together in continuous pairs. Clip pairs apart and assemble rows. Join rows to complete the quilt face.*

PROJECT: EASY COLOR, *HATTIE'S QUILT*
(Fig. 8-10; and see C-30 in the color section)

Overview: The blocks of this easy quilt are decorated by crayon and set with heat. Child-sized, it is quick to piece, assemble and quilt by machine. You can make a pile of fabric crayon drawings and choose the best or draw directly on the squares with fabric pastels.

Theme: Hattie Stroud, my six-year-old granddaughter, agreed happily to draw favorite things. It was near Christmas so decorated trees came to her mind. She drew her cat, Chessy, who came to inspect the crayons for edibility. She pictured her dad as a YMCA Indian Princess den chief. She likes grapes, apples, and strawberries, so they were added. As do most kindergarten kids, she made a turkey from her hand tracing.

Techniques: (1) Crayon transfer, pastel direct coloring; and (2) string-piecing.

Size: 38-1/2" x 50-1/2" (98cm x 126cm), block size 9-1/2" (24cm) square; sashings 2-1/2" (6cm).

Colors: Off-white background blocks; and pink, fuchsia, rust, and purple sashing.

On your quilt, select sashing and borders after the blocks are done so you can blend the colors. If you don't keep fabrics on hand, take the blocks to the fabric store to choose sashing. Light-colored sashing emphasizes the drawing more than the blocks. Bright colors bring out the crayon colors and block shapes. Printed sashing may distract from the drawings. Primary color may overwhelm the crayon colors.

Include the artist on the choice of sashings but limit the choices. Hattie liked the colors of a heavy-weight cotton with wild designs but it over-powered her drawings, so she made another choice . . . but grudgingly.

MATERIALS

Background: 1 yard (91cm) polished cotton (includes extra blocks).

Sashing and borders: 10" (25cm) each fuchsia, rust, and purple; and 3" (8cm) pink.

Backing: 1-1/2 yards (137cm) harmonizing fabric.

Bonded batting fiberfill: 38-1/2" x 50-1/2" (98cm x 128cm).

Thread: Matching for backing with invisible thread for top.

Tools and supplies: Crayola Fabric Crayons and/or Pentel Fabricfun Pastel Dye Sticks; and white paper, masking tape, an iron or press, a mat board for frame, a ruler, and pins.

Selecting Fabrics

The base fabric for this technique must accept the color well. Polished cotton works best. Glazed chintz works well but the surface filler may wash off. All-cotton is recommended by the manufacturer, but run a test strip to compare results. Buy extra fabric since you may ruin blocks or you may wish to shift them for design purposes.

PROCEDURE

Prepare the Fabric Blocks

1 Tear the blocks into squares. Divide 44" (112cm) fabric into 11" (28cm) squares with no waste. This allows for a good-sized seam allowance in case the design needs shifting.

Note: Fabric may be pulled off-grain at the mill so tearing gives accurate true-grain blocks, but it also may pull threads and pucker edges. Trim the puckered edges.

2 Iron each block, pulling it square, as needed. Pulling it later will distort the drawing.

Draw the Designs

Crayon Transfer Drawings

1 Provide a box of fabric crayons and a stack of white paper trimmed to size. We used typing paper trimmed to 8-1/2" x 9" (21.6cm x 23cm) for finished blocks 9-1/2" (24cm) square on Hattie's quilt.

2 Draw the designs on the white paper. Colors will alter some when heat-set and color choice is limited, so improvise. Remember that designs, especially letters, appear in reverse when ironed on the fabric. Make good solid lines that show well; however, fill in areas, such as faces, with softer color. Color in objects with lines relating to the shapes. Every-which-way lines will forever be that way. Even so, don't hamper creativity, yours or the child's. Praise the child or yourself. An artist needs to feel good about what's happening in order to keep going.

Drawing with Fabric Pastels

1 Provide fabric pastels, masking tape, and ironed and squared quilt blocks (to begin, choose light colors; experiment later).

2 Tape the quilt block to a smooth tabletop. Children often draw right to the edge, so draw a chalk seam line, or make a masking tape frame. The fabric must be smooth and taut or it will stretch and pucker during drawing.

3 Draw your design on the fabric as described previously. Use care because this does not erase. One color can be applied over another to mix them.

Press On the Colors

For the Crayon Transfer

1 Put absorbent paper on the ironing board. Lay the background block polished side up on the absorbent paper. Shake off any crayon bits and pin the drawing in place. You can combine two or three drawings on one block, as Hattie did, but make sure to trim away overlapping paper.

2 The best appliance for doing this is a press with steady heat. Images will smear or print twice if the paper moves during ironing, so use a hand iron with care. Use a hot iron setting or as noted on the instructions to press on the designs. Work in a ventilated room to avoid wax fumes.

3 Before removing the paper, lift up a corner of the design. If the image is hazy or soft, carefully realign and apply more heat to fully transfer. You can touch up drawings while the fabric is still hot from ironing. The colors will melt into the fabric. Apply more heat to set the added color.

For Fabric Pastels

1 Shake or brush off bits of pastel that rubbed off during the drawing process or these bits will print when ironed. Place papers or old sheeting under the drawing to absorb the wax released by heating. Put the drawn blocks face down on paper or fabric padding with absorbent paper on top.

2 Work in a ventilated room. Heat the iron to the cotton setting, or as hot as your fabric will take (a polycotton blend takes less heat). Press, changing absorbent paper until all the color is set.

Assemble the Quilt Pieces by Strip Piecing

Here's a technique for easy quilt assembly: If the quilt blocks and sashings are cut accurately and the fabrics have the same weight and stretch, the quilt can be assembled without seam line markings on the backs.

1 Measure and trim the blocks to exactly to 10-1/2" (26cm) square for 1/2" (1.5cm) seam allowances.

2 Measure and cut the sashing pieces to exactly 3-1/2" x 10-1/2" (8cm x 26cm).

3 Pick up the sashing and blocks in horizontal rows and stack them by rows, consulting Fig. 8-1, if necessary. This results in nine rows, five of sashing and corners and four of sashing and blocks.

4 To assemble by sewing machine, begin at the top row left. Align the three pairs of corners and border sashing. Feed the pairs into the machine without cutting the thread between. Keep seam allowances at exactly 1/2" (1.5cm). You will add the final corner later.

5 On row two, align three sashing and block pairs. Pin at the corners if the fabric shows any sign of shifting when sewn and remove pins before sewing over them. Or finger pin this way: align the sashing and block edges and feed the fabric into the sewing machine for 1" (2.5cm). Hold the unsewn seam end firmly and pull as you stitch. Don't pull so much that you override the feed dogs, just enough to keep the fabrics moving through evenly. Sew the pairs of sashing and blocks continuously.

6 Assemble by rows and keep them stacked separately. Or if you can keep track, sew the rest of the quilt in pair combinations continuously.

7 Clip the pairs apart and assemble the rows, adding the single corner or sashing at the row ends.

8 Sew each sashing row to each block row by matching and pinning seams. It is easiest to join rows by folding all seam allowances away from the stitching direction to stitch, but it's best to press seams away from the white blocks so they don't shadow through.

Finishing the Quilt

1 Iron the seam allowances flat. Stack the smoothed batting, the finished quilt face down, and the backing. Smooth and align the edges. Pin the layer edges together and sew the edges, leaving an opening to turn. Trim the corners and turn the quilt. Sew the opening closed with hidden stitching and press the edges.

2 Smooth the quilt flat and safety pin the layers together every 6" (15cm), avoiding seam lines.

3 Thread the sewing machine with bobbin thread matching the backing and invisible thread on top. Stitch in the ditch (along the sewn seam), pulling the seam enough before and in back of the needle to keep the backing from pleating. Sew all the horizontal seams first and then the verticals. Remove and restitch any puckered or tucked stitch lines.

4 Quilting within the squares is optional depending on use. For display, it probably isn't necessary. For use, it is recommended. Hand- or machine-stitch around the designs. The colors are permanent and washable, but they will dull, so shaking out is best for cleaning.

TEXTURES: ADDING A THIRD DIMENSION

Chapter Nine

As rich as a picture can be in two dimensions full of lines, flat shapes, and colors, there's yet another element—the dimension of depth. In pictorial quilting, a third dimension means everything from the texture of the fabrics through the mounds created by quilting layers to the actual volume of stuffed pieces.

This chapter tells about fabrics and how to sew fur and pile fabrics. It describes three methods of assembling quilt layers and tells about quilting techniques: hand and machine quilting; trapunto; and soft sculpture. The project features *Favorite Cats* (Fig. 9-1), a quilt made with assorted furry and textured fabrics.

FABRICS

Canvas to paint on is a traditional artist's medium. It is of a much lighter weight than wood or stone of the same size. It can be rolled into a tube or folded for transporting, unlike wood or stone. Canvas is readily available in linen, cotton, or synthetics in fine or coarsely woven textures. The fibers in these materials hold the paint colors well and can accept a needle for stitching.

Stitchery artists use fabrics to give a background for imagery. Fabric is flexible, so it can be cut, sewn, folded, and gathered. It comes in many weaves and textures and in a wide variety of colors. Some fabrics are absorbent; some hold warmth; some admit cooling breezes; some stretch; some are transparent; and some are thick and wooly. Most fabrics are readily available at reasonable cost and are easy to manipulate. Use good quality fabrics to make good pieces.

Fabrics appear in every part of our homes from bed linens to dish towels, drapery walls, upholstery, clothing, and more. For this reason, fabrics are a familiar material to use. Quilts usually project a friendly image, a softness to cuddle you. In addition, they can embellish the necessary expanse of a bed with color, designs, and texture. Paintings, by contrast, are often viewed with suspicion since artists are committed by nature to trying something new, and this unsettles viewers. Fibers are a friendly medium, so many use this format to make their art, taking quilts up off the beds and putting them up on the walls.

Susan Shie and James Acord created *The World of the Wondrous: A Green Quilt* (Fig. 9-2). They say, "This quilt is at heart a simple 'nine-patch' of nine painted

9-1. Favorite Cats, 61" x 81" (155cm x 206cm), combines fur fabrics, velveteens, loop mohair, and wools in a textured wall quilt. Directions to make this project come at the end of the chapter.

9-2. The World of the Wondrous: A Green Quilt, 72" x 75" (183cm x 191cm), by Susan Shie and James Acord, has visual and actual texture with added leather masks, soft-sculptured vegetables, and more. Photo: Photography Unlimited, Wooster, Ohio.

fabric scenarios, although the 3-D appliqué tends to deny this simplicity." In fact, this wall-hung quilt makes its statement as strongly as a painting. The base is a canvas fabric drawn on directly with a Rub-A-Dub laundry marker for permanent images. Shapes within these lines were painted with permanent Deka Fabric Paint, which must be heat-set and produces fumes, so a respirator should be worn.

Quilting the painted fabric to a background fabric gives it added dimension. More dimension comes with the addition of tooled acrylic-painted leather pieces, metal beads, shells, pennies, wooden and metal masks, fabric bean pods (by artist Lisa Kane), and Sculpy pieces (a clay that fires at 275 degrees in a kitchen oven). The artists aim to illuminate the lives of the family that commissioned the piece.

Favorite Cats (Fig. 9-1) is a nine-patch quilt that uses the nostalgic friendliness of quilting as part of its message. It was designed laid out flat, as it might appear on a bed with three of the cats viewed from above. However, this perspective was limiting. Not all the cats wanted to lie flat, or even stay on their blocks, so a mixed perspective was used. Consistency came from imagery and texture of the fabrics.

Kinds of Fabrics

1. Plain Weaves: Plain weaves are the most popular for traditional quilting. The tighter the weave, the greater the dimensional stability of the fabric (it doesn't pull out of shape). Medium-weight, firmly woven fabrics in cotton or polycotton include muslin, calico, broadcloth, percale, and others. All-cotton fabric is easier to hand sew, but a polycotton blend is less apt to wrinkle; see Fig. 7-3 in chapter 7 for a diagram of the weave.

Fabrics in the stores are usually arranged by weave and fiber content, such as cotton, silk, wool, and so on. Plain weaves come in assorted weights and textures. Heavyweight fabrics include artist canvas, art linen for embroidery, denim for study sports clothing, and tweed for wool suiting. A canvas weight for background or backing is ideal for machine embroidery because it does not pucker under the pull of the stitches.

Other plain weaves include such fabrics as: silk in lightweight, tightly packed fibers for brilliance in dye colors; organdy with loosely packed, stiffened fibers for embroidery; or some metallics in tightly woven coated fabrics for novelty. Rarely used for quilting are loosely woven, soft, plain weaves such as limp cheesecloth or open-weave drapery, which generally lack dimensional stability.

2. Twill and Lustrous Weaves: To show the luster or sheen of the fiber, some fabrics are woven with long overshots. This means that the fibers on the fabric surface pass over several fibers before interlacing again (see Fig. 7-3 in chapter 7). Long overshot fabric edges can fray during the appliqué process but covering the appliqué piece with a clear plastic bag and making a wide satin-stitch through it and over the fabric edges will help control this. On these fabrics, fused backing helps with stability but only partly with fraying overshots.

In Joyce Marquess Carey's *Money Talks* (see C-31 in the color section), two different metallics, a coated firm weave and a satin weave with long-overshots, are used to represent dimes and pennies. She straight-stitched the low-relief sculptured details of a dime through the metallic fabric and under layers to create a dimensional effect.

3. Elaborate or Textured Weaves: These weaves include tapestries, brocades, Jacquards, matelassé, and double cloth. The background for the dime in Joyce Marquess Carey's piece mentioned above is a two-tone elaborate weave that provides subtle color and texture. These fabrics always look different on the reverse side, a characteristic you can take advantage of since the colors will relate. These, too, will have overshots, but most will be tightly woven and sturdy. Take care of fraying at the edges as mentioned. Margaret Cusack used a wondrous collection of elegant fabrics in *Celebrity Stockings* (see Fig. 8-5 in chapter 8).

4. Nappy and Furry Fabrics: Pile fabrics have vertical fibers projecting up from a woven (or knitted) backing. Some are trimmed evenly (velveteen or velvet), some in rows (corduroy), and some loosely (fur-like fabrics). Usually the pile or loops are woven into the fabric, but sometimes the surface is brushed hard to raise a nap (loosely woven wools). All of these take care in handling in order to sew them. Pile fabrics slide under pressure and must be held securely, not by more pressure but by hand basting, by careful pinning, or by using a sewing-machine roller foot. Loop or long-haired fabrics (terry cloth, mohair, fake furs) may catch in the presser foot so brush long pile out of the way as you sew and use a closed front presser foot or put tape across the front of your presser foot.

5. Other Types of Fabrics: It's amazing how many kinds of fabrics you'll see in a full fabric store. And then styles change, inventions and developments occur, and you see even more different kinds. Textured fabrics can have crinkly yarns (crepe), slub threads (raw silk), ripples (seersucker with alternate rows of shrunken threads), stretchy yarns (for bathing suits or bicycle pants), and non-fraying construction (Ultrasuede, felt, fulled wool).

Mixing Fabrics

Traditional quilters stick to tabby weave, medium-weight cotton fabrics because the fabrics match in thickness, flexibility, surface reflection, texture, and colors. They look related and are. They will all handle the same when sewn. Even so, you can use any fabric that appeals for a pictorial quilt, although this comes with a warning. While you increase the range of texture and color possibilities with mixed or unusual fabrics, you also increase the problems. For example, a heavyweight fabric sewn to a light one will pull the light one out of shape when hung. You need to add backing to the light fabric to equalize the two fabrics. You can cope with most technical sewing problems of this type by backing, basting, and stabilizing.

A bigger problem arises in relating the visual weight of different fabrics. Using fur fabrics with gingham is hard to make work. The cotton colors are light and crisp while the fur is fuzzy and visually heavy. A light-colored fur or a darker gingham could pull them together visually. It is not so much the fabric type as the color, texture, and visual weight that need to relate—relate, but not necessarily match.

Have fun and be audacious in mixing fabrics, but be true to the character of the materials. Velveteen has a depth of surface that seems to require equally lustrous or textured fabrics as companions. The *Favorite Cats* quilt uses a mix of fur fabrics, velveteens, wools, denim, linen, and even polycotton. The light-colored fabrics are heavy textured while the lightweight fabrics are heavy colored, grayed dark blue, for example. A general rule on combining fabrics is asking yourself if you would wear them together. Or, depending on the character of the piece you are doing, would a zany character wear them together?

Sewing Fur and Pile Fabrics

1. Fur Fabrics: Fur fabrics are harder and easier to appliqué than nonpile fabrics. Knitted-back furs are stretchy and must be held down securely to stitch. Woven-back fur fabrics have greater stability, but the trend has been toward knit-backed robe fabric because it drapes more softly. Some fur fabric backing has been coated, which stiffens and stabilizes it. (Putting fusibles on the back of furs is not recommended.) Fur fabrics should be cut from the back with a single-edge razor blade or with short snips of the scissors slid through the pile. Even when you are careful, the fur will fly, so wear a pollen mask when sewing furs.

2. Appliquéing Fur Fabrics

1. Trace the template or pattern, minus the seam allowances, on the backing and trace. Trim 1/8" (3mm) outside this line for seamed joinings or on the line for appliqué pieces.

2. To hold fur fabrics in place, use plastic-headed 1-1/2" (4cm) pins across the stitch line, or you may be able to tape the pieces in place (but don't leave the tape on for any length of time).

3. Ease the pressure on the presser foot of your sewing machine to allow for the increased thickness and set it for a medium to wide zigzag stitch. Choose matching thread for an invisible outline.

4. Stitch along the edge with the outermost swing of the zigzag at the edge of the fur. Brush the fur away from the stitch line as you sew to keep it out of the presser foot and so it will overlap the seamed edge later. Pull out the holding

9-3. *The long-haired cat from the Favorite Cats quilt was trimmed like a real pet to create its features.*

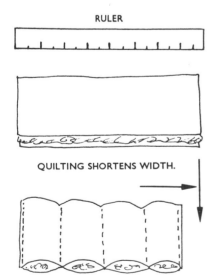

RULER

QUILTING SHORTENS WIDTH.

9-4. *Quilting stitches make a flat fabric into hills and valleys, shortening the width and length of a quilted piece.*

pins as you come to them. When completed, brush to pull any caught pile out from the stitching so it can lay naturally.

3. Trimming Fur Fabrics

1. The cat in Fig. 9-3 has had a haircut. If not, you wouldn't be able to see its eyes or legs. To do this, appliqué the cat in place on the background, as above.

2. Use sharp scissors to clip hairs away from the face and contour the lines of the leg. Clip cautiously. It won't grow back.

3. When you have trimmed to the shape you want, hand- or machine-sew demarcation lines around the nose and mouth, on the ears, and around the leg. Ear lines are needle-punched in a fine wool yarn. Don't insert the eyes before this point because you can't machine sew lines close to them. Plastic eyes have a post on the back for a lock washer.

To Sew Pile Fabrics

1. Velveteen and corduroy will shed pile when torn or cut. Trace the template on the back or pin the pattern to the front to keep it in place. Be sure to leave an adequate seam allowance of at least 1/2" (13mm) or more when cutting to avoid fraying. Both fabrics also slide out of place when pressure is applied crushing the pile sideways. For this reason they must be secured well before stitching.

2. To sew, ease the pressure on the presser foot. (A roller foot accessory works well for long straight seams but not for maneuvering.) Hand baste or use silk pins across the stitch line. To appliqué, use the "stitch through the pattern/trim later" technique from chapter 7.

3. Be careful not to trim seam allowances too close after stitching seams or basting appliqué pieces and do use a wide satin-stitch when appliquéing. For hand appliqué use Fray Check to keep the material from raveling.

Adding Surface Texture

Satin-stitching on the edges usually looks better with short-pile fur or velveteen than with long pile fur. Stitching within fur fabrics quilts them, creating a dimensional effect. Surface stitching of many kinds can be added to textured fabrics for interesting effects. You can hand embroider, machine embroider, or needle-punch added designs. Buttons, ribbons, beads, and other small objects can be sewn on.

QUILTING

The Quilting Process

Additional texturing comes from the quilting process. Layering adds stability to fabrics, supporting them from sagging. The stitching that bonds the layers creates a three-dimensional pattern, and lighting from the side brings this out. In Mary Gentry's colorful *Chicago Community Gardens* (see C-28 in the color section), she used both hand and machine quilting to make each shape stand out. C-32 shows the reverse side of the sunflower and the dimensional effect achieved by machine-sewn lines that follow the details.

1. Quilting Draws Up the Fabric: Instead of lying flat it now forms hills and valleys (Fig. 9-4). This shortens the length the fabric will cover. Quilting stitches pull in and decrease the over-all dimensions of a piece. Plan an evenly balanced quilting pattern on a layered piece so it will draw in consistently. Quilting lines that are sewn horizontally will shorten a piece but not diminish width. Vertical stitch lines decrease the width without shortening it.

If different sections are quilted in different directions, the piece will be uneven. Mary Gentry uses this to advantage, quilting closely in several directions causing the center of the flower to have a sculptured look (see C-32 in the color section).

2. Fillers: Natural unspun fibers, such as cotton and wool, were commonly used as quilt fillers. The lofty loose fibers trapped air and provided warmth. Cotton had a tendency to flatten and wool to felt when washed, so something better was needed. Polyester fiberfill stuffing was the answer: no more bunching, shifting, or migrating filler and no more pre-shrinking the cotton. Then something even better was added: batts, formerly available only in loose fibers of fiberfill or cotton, could now be bonded into one continuous piece—and stay that way! This means quilts needn't be quilted with so many stitches to hold the filler in place.

Fabric stores and quilt catalogs offer a wide range of fillers. Loose fiberfill for toy or trapunto stuffing comes in bags of various sizes and grades of quality. Batts come in various sizes and thicknesses. One fiberfill batt is bonded so firmly it resembles a felt blanket. You can use a blanket for quilt filler and not even need a backing, unless you wanted one. In the past, and even now, thrifty quilters have made one quilt right over another when the first showed too much wear. Choose a filler that meets your needs. Wool, cotton, fiberfill, and silk batts are available in thin to thick weights and even in a dark color for dark fabrics.

3. Hoops: For hand quilting round hoops up to 24" (61cm) across cover a good-size area, but it may be difficult to reach the center. Oval hoops of various sizes take care of this, and some come on stands to ease the weight. A half-oval is now available for doing edges. Handy, too, is a PVC plastic tube and corner hoop set that makes a square, convenient for quilting block motifs. Full-width quilting frames take up a lot of space, but many hands can join in and the quilt comes out smooth.

If you like the character of hand quilting, machine-assemble the quilt and finish with handquilting, as quilters have been doing since the invention of the sewing machine in the mid-1800s. Machine-embroidery hoops generally won't work for layered quilting. Read below for machine-quilting techniques.

Three Ways To Make Quilt Layers

1. Traditional: Because quilting can distort a piece, traditional quilts (Fig. 9-5) are made in a standard order: layers are assembled, are secured together, then quilted, and an edging is added last of all.

   1. Create the top (quilt face) by whatever means you prefer: piecing, appliqué, or embroidery.

   2. Lay the backing face down on a large flat surface. Make sure it is squared so that the grain runs true and there are no wrinkles. Tape it to a hard surface or pin it to the rug to keep it square.

   3. Spread the filler smoothly on the backing (being careful not to stretch bonded batting because it will contract later), and trim off the extra batting around the edges.

TRADITIONAL ASSEMBLY OF QUILT

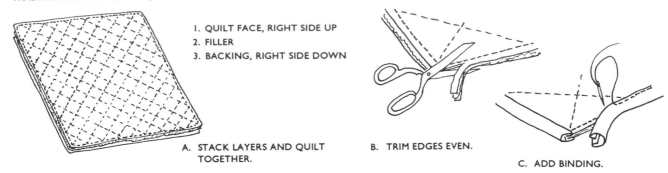

1. QUILT FACE, RIGHT SIDE UP
2. FILLER
3. BACKING, RIGHT SIDE DOWN

A. STACK LAYERS AND QUILT TOGETHER.

B. TRIM EDGES EVEN.

C. ADD BINDING.

9-5. *Assembling quilt layers by the traditional method means stacking the layers, sewing the quilting pattern to join the layers and then adding a binding over the raw edges to finish.*

4. Spread the finished quilt face smoothly over the two layers face up.

5. Secure the layers together with basting stitches or safety pins at close intervals, such as 6" (15cm) apart. Sometimes a strip of muslin is sewn all around the edge for attaching the quilting frame or hoop. At this point, the quilt is ready to hand or machine quilt.

9-6. *The quilting stitches joining layers become an important part of the pattern in Big Apple Circus, 47" x 54" (119cm x 137cm), by Margit Echols. Some quilt parts are movable—the tent flaps and the elephant ears. Photo: Myron Miller.*

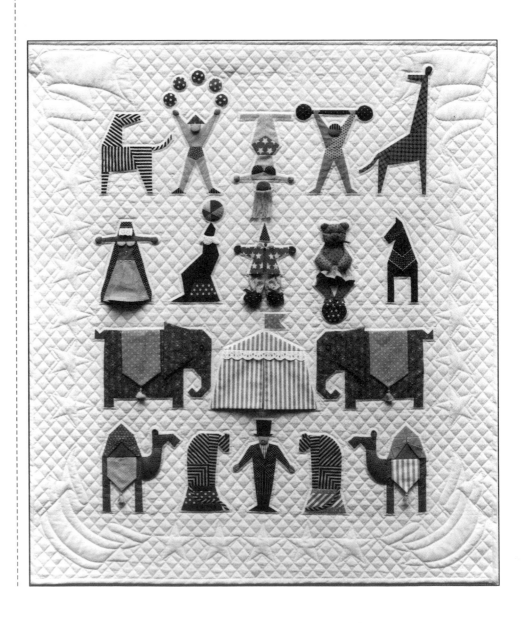

6. Traditionally, quilting stitches are sewn from the center to keep the piece even. When quilting is completed, measure and cut straight sides and square the corners. Trim the edges evenly, removing the muslin strip.

7. Sew a narrow binding strip over the raw edge to complete, leaving room in the strip for mitering at the corners.

A beautiful example of traditional-style quilting was done by Margit Echols in her *Big Apple Circus* wall quilt (Fig. 9-6). She has interspersed stars and banners in a diamond-grid quilting pattern, providing an important element of design. The delightful stuffed circus figures on the quilt have the same crisp squared-off look for a geometric consistency.

2. Envelope Method: In this method (Fig. 9-7), the layers are assembled reversed, an edge seam is sewn, and the quilt is turned right side out before quilting. I prefer this method because it avoids the narrow edge strip as a design element. Further, the quilt looks completed long before it is, while it awaits a long winter evening for hand quilting or an energetic day for machine quilting.

　I. Lay the bonded batting on a large open space and smooth but do not stretch it. (Bonded batting is necessary for this method).

　2. Lay the completed top face up on the batting and carefully smooth it in place. Measure to make sure it is squared and not askew. Tape it to a hard surface or pin it to the rug to keep it square.

　3. Trim the batting edges to size and place pins every 6" (15cm) to 12" (30.5cm) to secure these two layers.

　4. Lay the backing face down on the quilt face, trim to size, and pin around the edges with pins placed at right angles to the stitch line.

　5. Starting on the quilt bottom edge 12" (30.5cm) away from the corner, machine-sew around the entire quilt, ending 24" (61cm) from the beginning to leave an opening 24" (61cm) wide for turning.

Note: If you want to make a rod pocket to hang the quilt, leave a 4" (10cm) opening at the top on both sides. Details for this appear at the end of chapter 2, Fig. 2-12.

　6. Trim across the corners (except for rod pocket corners) and trim away the filler seam allowances.

　7. Turn the quilt right side out and baste or press the edges. Machine sew the batting to the quilt face across the opening to keep the batting from shifting at that point. Hand sew the opening closed with hidden stitching.

　8. Lay the quilt flat and squared. Repin the safety pins through all layers and hand or machine quilt the layers.

3. Strip Quilting: This method (Fig. 9-8) can be done by hand or machine. Sections of the quilt top are completed, layered, and quilted and then joined to other sections. This allows for working with smaller and less bulky parts of the quilt.

　I. Piece sections of the quilt (block and sashing, for example) into strips, horizontal or vertical, leaving seam allowances around the perimeter of these top strips.

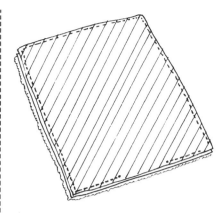

A. STACK LAYERS
 I. BACKING, RIGHT SIDE DOWN
 2. QUILT FACE, RIGHT SIDE UP
     (FACING BACKING)
 3. FILLER
 4. SEAM EDGES LEAVING OPENING
     TO TURN.

B. CLIP CORNERS. TRIM EDGES.

QUILTING HOOP

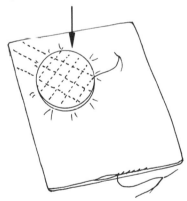

C. TURN QUILT,
 SEW OPENING CLOSED.
 QUILT THE LAYERS TOGETHER.

9-7. To assemble quilt layers by the envelope method, stack the layers with the filler first, the quilt face up, and the backing face down on top, seam the edges, trim and turn, and then quilt. This allows for including a rod pocket to display and needs no edge binding.

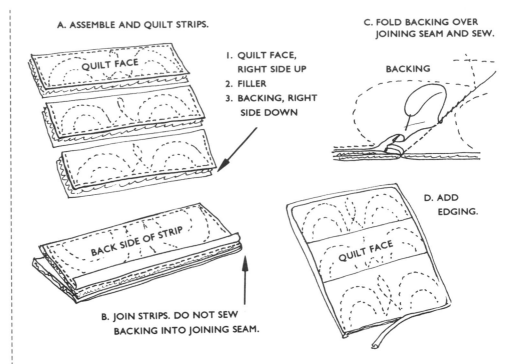

A. ASSEMBLE AND QUILT STRIPS.

QUILT FACE

1. QUILT FACE, RIGHT SIDE UP
2. FILLER
3. BACKING, RIGHT SIDE DOWN

C. FOLD BACKING OVER JOINING SEAM AND SEW.

BACKING

D. ADD EDGING.

QUILT FACE

BACK SIDE OF STRIP

B. JOIN STRIPS. DO NOT SEW BACKING INTO JOINING SEAM.

9-8. *To assemble quilt layers by the strip method involves quilting the layers before the quilt is assembled. Finished strips are sewn together with the backing stitched over the joinings. Usually, an edge binding is added to finish the quilt.*

2. For the first strip, lay out the backing face down, place the filler strip on the backing, and add the top strip face up to this. Smooth the layers and baste or pin them together.

3. Hand or machine quilt the strip layers except for 1" (2.5cm) on the long edges.

4. Repeat all of these three steps for each successive strip.

5. When the top strips are quilted, lay the second strip face to face with the first. Fold back a 1" (2.5cm) strip of backing on the second strip along the unquilted area.

6. Pin the two strips together along the seam line, excluding the folded backing, and stitch with a 1/2" (13mm) seam allowance. You will be sewing through all three layers on one strip and the top and filler of the other.

7. Trim off the filler from both sections along this seam line and tuck in the seam allowances toward the folded backing. Hand or machine stitch the backing in place. Repeat for each row until the quilt is assembled.

8. To finish, measure and trim the edges evenly, pin and sew a binding around the edges (leaving space for the corner miter), fold the binding over, and hem in place.

Quilting the Quilt

1. Hand quilting: To hand quilt, fix the area to be quilted in a hoop. Use a short running stitch or stab-stitch to quilt, one hand on top and the other under to guide the needle. Running stitches gathered several at a time on the needle can only be done with soft fabrics, thin filler, and the quilt not too tightly stretched in the hoop. Stab-stitching means poking each stitch up and down individually, which results in close stitches. Quilt the area within the hoop, carefully refit the hoop pair to another area, and sew. Do this until the surface is quilted. Quilting stitches sewn 1/8" (3mm) in from the seam line provide a decorative line of stitches. Stitching on the seam line, called "in the ditch," results in hidden stitches.

2. Machine Quilting: Quilting by sewing machine is harder to control but faster (see C-15 in the color section). However, it is faster only if you sew carefully, not if you must spend time picking out stitches.

1. Begin with the quilting layers assembled and pinned or basted as described above. Plan to quilt in long straight rows if possible. If not, plan to quilt a section across the quilt or lengthwise in which you can sew consistently in the same direction.

2. Fold or roll the quilt to expose the area you plan to quilt and minimize the bulk of the rest as you put it through the sewing machine. Use bicycle clips, clip clothes pins or large safety pins to fold the roll in place. In the center you may need to roll it from both ends.

3. Use a clear or matching thread and stitch in the ditch along seam lines, unless you want exposed stitch lines. For quilting that shows, you can use straight or decorative programmed machine stitches.

4. To stitch the seam, hold the quilt firmly in front of and behind the needle to keep the backing from tucking, puckering, or going askew. Check the back immediately to see what happened. If the safety pins aren't spaced closely enough to hold securely, straight pin each line just before stitching and remove pins as you come to them.

5. Reposition the rolled part of the quilt as needed and stitch each quilting row. Check each row on the back as you complete sewing it, just in case something horrible is happening, and more than one row is pulled out of shape.

6. Some say you should stitch each row in the same direction in case of any pulling. I say you must be accurate enough so it doesn't matter which way you stitch. If the top shows angled wrinkles, take the stitching out, repin, and restitch.

3. Trapunto: In this technique, certain areas are stuffed to give added dimension. This can be done in several ways:

1. Italian trapunto was originally done by sewing design areas in two layers of fabric. The threads of the backing fabrics were pried apart, stuffing tucked in, and the threads pushed back into place.

2. For the slit technique, quilt two layers of fabric together or add additional trapunto to a three-layer quilted piece. Cut slits in the back of the areas outlined by stitching and stuff. Sew the slit closed.

3. Place a layer of stuffing over the area to be stuffed. Lay fabric over this. Pin the fabric down, and machine stitch around the edges, or lay a pattern over it and sew through the pattern. Trim the seam allowances off, and satin-stitch over the stitch line (see chapter 1, Fig. 1-15).

4. Soft Sculpture: Picture quilters can and do try anything. Once they start adding dimension, they soon come to full-round soft sculpture. Mary Gentry added three-dimensional parts to her wall quilt piece (see C-34 in the color section). As charming as the piece seems with work-stocking monkeys, it is actually a war protest piece. The three monkeys see no evil, hear no evil, and speak no evil as the flames of war engulf them and planes fly around. Symbolic yellow ribbons await the soldiers' return.

Mary Gentry uses several traditional homey sewing techniques to contrast the horrors of war with the innocence of home arts. She gathered and smocked the red fire at the bottom, and used rhinestones on black at the top to show the tracer bullets over Baghdad that unforgettable night when the Persian Gulf War began.

Sue Pierce plays an optical game in her *Escape From Block Nine* (see C-33 in the color section). The red block is flat in the upper left corner and grows increasingly three-dimensional toward the bottom. Finally, it leaps off the quilt to sit on its own Plexiglas stand in front of the quilt.

El Tigre mask is a copy of an authentic Mexican mask I found in a book and coveted for my small mask collection. I made one for myself from quilted layers and then stuffed it (Fig. 9-9).

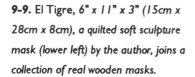

9-9. El Tigre, 6" x 11" x 3" (15cm x 28cm x 8cm), a quilted soft sculpture mask (lower left) by the author, joins a collection of real wooden masks.

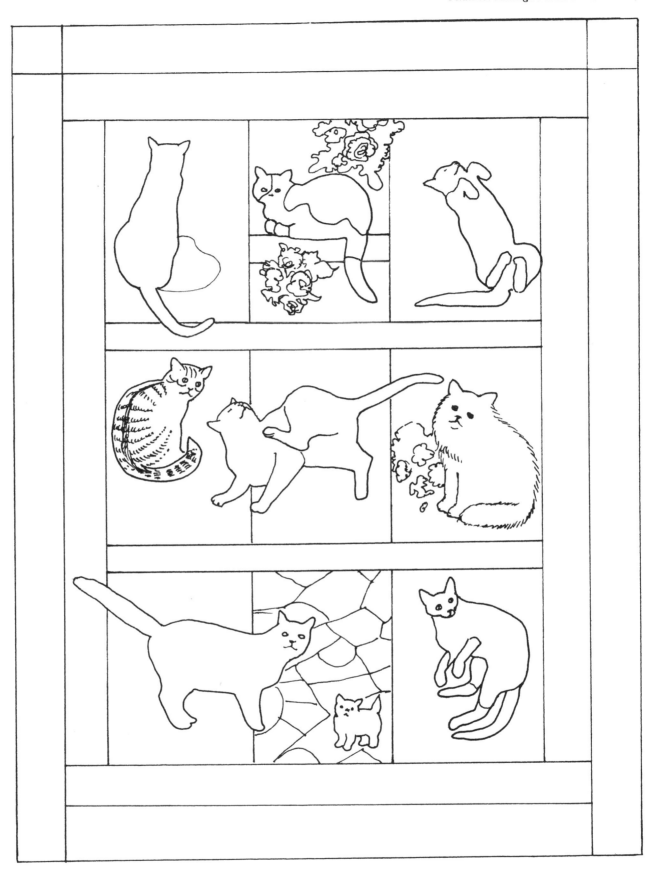

9-10. Here is the pattern for the
Favorite Cats quilt. Scale it up to size.

PROJECT: SEW FUR FABRICS, *FAVORITE CATS*
(Fig. 9-10; and see C-35 in the color section)

Overview: This quilt features cats in appropriate fur or textured fabrics appliquéd onto the quilt blocks. Where cats overlap other blocks or sashing, their appliqué stitching was completed after the piecing seams were sewn. Blocks and sashings are made of related napped or woolly fabrics in earth tones.

Theme: Cats I've known and loved are memorialized on this wall-hung quilt. Well, one was a not-so-favorite cat, but she was pictorial.

Techniques: (1) Zigzag appliqué, (2) strip assembly, and (3) blanket backing.

Size: 61" x 81" (155cm x 206cm).

Block size: 14" x 19" (36cm x 48cm), varies in size slightly.

FABRIC AND YARDAGES

To maintain the furry softness of cats, fur fabrics, cottons, velvets and other textured fabrics were used.

Blocks: 15" x 20" (38cm x 51cm) each; blue denim, rust wool synthetic, taupe synthetic linen, rose-brown printed velveteen, muted deep blue polycotton, mauve velveteen and mauve print velvet, oatmeal nubby synthetic, tan/rust/black-printed velveteen, and nubby denim-blue synthetic.

Cats: Fake fur fabric 1/2" (13mm) pile; 1/2 yard (46cm) black; 10" x 15" (25cm x 38cm) each of gray, white, brown, cream, and taupe; 1-1/2" (3.8cm) pile fake fur; 10" x 15" (25cm x 38cm) white with brown tips; and 15" x 15" (38cm x 38cm) rust loop mohair.

Sashings: Rose-brown velveteen; two pieces 78" x 6" (198cm x 15cm) and one piece 54" x 6" (137cm x 15cm); dark brown print velvet 54" x 6" (137cm x 15cm); two pieces gray-brown synthetic wool 64" x 6" (162cm x 15cm); two pieces 54" x 6" (137cm x 15cm) gray synthetic wool 44" x 3-1/4" (112cm x 8cm); and two pieces lavender velveteen, one piece 48" x 3-1/4" (122cm x 8cm) and one 21" x 2-1/4" (53cm x 6cm).

Added background pieces: 1/4 yard (23cm) rose/maroon/taupe velveteen in three pieces, and brown-print velvet 16" x 4" (41cm x 10cm).

PROCEDURE

Patterns (Fig. 9-11)

1 Enlarge and trace the patterns on paper. No seam allowances were used. If you plan to hand sew, add seam allowances.

2 To make your own patterns draw sketches of your cats in a variety of positions, or take photos of your cat, project, and trace them for patterns (see chapter 5).

Cut Out the Quilt Pieces

1 Measure and trim the blocks to the sizes you want or as given.

2 Cut out the fur cats. Trace the template on the reverse side of the fake fur and use a razor blade or short snips of the scissors to cut them out.

3 If your color scheme varies from that given, lay the quilt out as you think the pieces look best and shift blocks and sashing around to balance visually.

Appliqué the Cats
(See about sewing furs earlier in this chapter.)

1 On blocks where the cat is wholly contained, appliqué the cat to the background. Use stabilizing paper or fabric on the back, if needed.

2 Where a cat overlaps the next block, seam the two blocks together and then complete appliquéing the cat.

3 Where a cat overlaps the sashing, leave the cat loose 1/2" (13mm) from the block edge for seam allowance. Assemble the blocks into three rows.

Assemble the Quilt Face

1 Machine sew the center two rows of sashing to the three rows of cats to complete a central square. Where a cat tail overlaps, sew the seam, pin the tail in place, and zigzag the appliqué in place.

2 Align, pin, and sew the sashing in this order: the side inner sashings, the bottom inner sashing, the bottom and top dark brown sashings, and the side sashings.

Backing

1 This quilt has a taupe plush blanket for its backing. Lay the blanket face down on a large flat area and smooth.

2 Lay the quilt top face down on the blanket. Smooth it and make sure it is squared.

3 Measure and draw a seam line around on the back side of the top, which is up.

4 Trim the blanket to size and pin all around the edges at right angles to the seam line. Machine-stitch all around the edges leaving a 24" (61cm) opening to turn.

5 Trim the corners and seam allowances, turn, and sew the opening closed. Press the edges, pin the layers together, and quilt.

6 Quilting within the squares is optional, depending on its use. For display, it may not be necessary because of sturdy fabric weight and weaves, although unquilted areas do sag in time. For use, quilting is recommended. Hand- or machine-stitch around the cats.

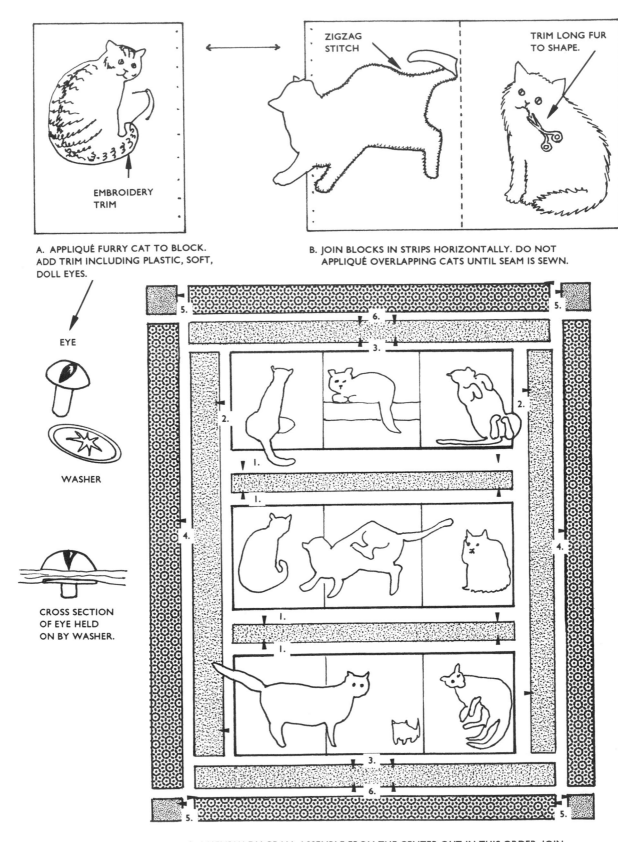

A. APPLIQUÉ FURRY CAT TO BLOCK.
ADD TRIM INCLUDING PLASTIC, SOFT,
DOLL EYES.

B. JOIN BLOCKS IN STRIPS HORIZONTALLY. DO NOT
APPLIQUÉ OVERLAPPING CATS UNTIL SEAM IS SEWN.

ZIGZAG STITCH

TRIM LONG FUR TO SHAPE.

EMBROIDERY TRIM

EYE

WASHER

CROSS SECTION
OF EYE HELD
ON BY WASHER.

C. ASSEMBLY DIAGRAM. ASSEMBLE FROM THE CENTER OUT IN THIS ORDER: JOIN
(1) BLOCKS TO HORIZONTAL SASHING, THEN (2) SIDE SASHING, ADD (3) BOTTOM
AND TOP SASHINGS, (4) SIDE FRAMES, (5) TOP AND BOTTOM FRAMES TO CORNERS,
AND LAST, TOP AND BOTTOM FRAMES/CORNERS.

9-11. Here are the instructions for making the cat quilt.

FAREWELL

❖

My part is done. I've packed everything I could fit into this book of limited pages to help you make picture quilts. You now know the process artists go through to get their ideas, to design their works, and to create pictorial space. You can do it, too. The secrets of tools and techniques used to draw, transfer images, create grids, make design patterns, and apply colors are yours to use. Many methods of sewing, embroidering, piecing, quilting, and appliquéing are described for you to consider. Give some of these ideas a try.

I did. I've even tried ideas that came to me as I was writing about these various quilts and projects. In one, using a color copy of an artist's wonderful stitchery, I cut the copy into squares, reassembled the pieces, and used photo transfer gel to adhere them to canvas. Then I machine embroidered and framed the result.

My grandchildren as well—who keep a toy basket in the studio along with my artist "toys"—felt inspired by this book in process. Using leftover quilt patches, four-year-old Bradley sat on my lap and carefully guided the fabric while six-year-old Hattie sat under the machine and squeezed the foot pedal on command. Bradley found a gorgeous variegated metallic Sulky thread and wanted to try all the pre-set stitches. The kids elbowed each other to switch places until their small pillows were done. They're proud of their creations and are ready to try something else. I hope you feel inspired to make something too.

You may be one of those people like my sister who read crafts books just for the pleasure. "You know nobody is going to try that," a friend said about some of the complicated quilts, "They just love to look at the pictures." She's right. The works contributed by the artists included here have certainly given me great pleasure. Yet you never know when the wonderful mix of images and ideas that go into your head as you read this book are going to pop out in the vision of a picture quilt that you must make.

Good luck with the idea now shimmering into reality in your mind. It's time for your part now. Start little or start big—but do begin. And I wish I could see the quilt when you've finished.

Carolyn Vosburg Hall

Sources

Books, Magazines, and Mail-Order Catalogues:

Books on Designing
The Art of Hand Lettering, Helen Witzkow, Dover
Design Dialogue, Jerry Samuelson and Jack Stoops, Davis Publications
Perspective, Victor Perard, Pitman Art Books
The Principles of Pattern, Richard Proctor, Van Nostrand Reinhold
See and Draw, Karl V. Larsen, Davis Publications
Time-Life Nature series, Time-Life Publishers

Books by the Author—Carolyn Vosburg Hall
The A to Z Soft Toy Book, Prentice Hall
Friendship Quilts by Hand and Machine, Chilton
The Sewing Machine Crafts Book, Van Nostrand Reinhold
Soft Sculpture, Davis Publications
Stitched and Stuffed Art, Doubleday
The Teddy Bear Crafts Book, Prentice Hall

Chilton Books on Quilting
The Complete Book of Machine Embroidery, Robbie Fanning
Contemporary Quilting Techniques, Pat Cairns
Machine Quilting, Nancy Moore
Putting on the Glitz, Sandra Hatch and Ann Boyce
Quilt as You Go, Sandra Millet
Quilting the World Over, Willow Ann Soltow
Rotary Cutting, Donna Poster
Speed Cut Quilts, Donna Poster
Textile Arts, Multicultural Traditions, Margo Singer and Mary Spyrou
and other Chilton books on quilting and knowing your sewing machine

Books on Quilting and Related Arts
American Patchwork and Quilting, Better Homes and Gardens
Celebrating the Stitch, Barbara Lee Smith, A Threads Book–Taunton Press
The Fiber Arts Design Books #1, 2, 3, 4, Hastings House Publisher
Remember Me, Linda Otto Lipsett, Quilt Digest Press

Catalogues and Sources for Supplies
Artograph, Minneapolis, Minnesota 55417, *for opaque projector.*
Blue-Printables, 1504 #7 Industrial Way, Belmont, California 94002, phone 1-800-356-0445, *for light sensitive muslin squares.*

Clotilde's Catalogue of Sewing Notions, 1909 SW First Avenue, Fort Lauderdale, Florida 33315-2100, 1-800-772-2891, *for sewing supplies and tools, and sewing videos and books.*

DMI Industries, toll free 1-800-312-1817 (Michigan); 1-800-321-1818 (outside Michigan), *for artist drafting supplies.*

Dritz, P.O. Box 5028, Spartanburg, South Carolina 29304, *for sewing supplies, pins, Iron-off to clean irons, and so on.*

Fairfield, P.O. Box 1130, Danbury, Connecticut 06813, *for quilt fillers.*

Hancock Fabrics, 3841 Hinkleville Road, Paducah, Kentucky 42001, 1-800-626-2723, ext 456, *for Gingher scissors, notions, and so on.*

Hinterberg Design, 2100 Northwestern Avenue, West Bend, Wisconsin 53095, *for quilting hoops and frames.*

Keepsake Quilting—The Quilter's Wish Book, Department TMC24, Dover Street, P.O. Box 1459, Meridith, New Hampshire 03253, *for quilting supplies, fabrics, tools, and more.*

Nancy's Notions, Department 9810, P.O. Box 683, Beaver Dam, Wisconsin 53916-0683, 1-800-833-0690, *for free mail-order catalogue.*

National Thread and Supply Company, 695 Red Oak Road, Stockbridge, California 30281, 1-800-331-7600, ext. A-1192, *for irons, ironing boards, sewing furniture, threads, cutters, rotary cutters, and cutting mats.*

Photographer's Formulary, P.O. Box 5105, Missoula, Montana 59806, *for blue print chemicals and kits.*

Rupert, Gibbon and Spider, P.O. Box 425, Healdsburg, California 95448, *for dyes and dyeable fabrics.*

Threads

Coats and Clark, 30 Patewood Plaza, Greenville, South Carolina 29615.

Madeira Marketing, 600 East Ninth, Michigan City, Indiana 46360, *for a variety of Tanne threads.*

Seerite, Testrite Instrument Company, 135 Monroe Street, Newark, New York 07105.

Sulky, 3113-D Broadpoint Drive, Harbor Heights, Florida 33983, 1-800-874-4115, *for elegant decorative threads.*

Magazines on Sewing

The Creative Machine, Open Chain Publishing, P.O. Box 2634-NL, Menlo Park, California 94026, *for Robbie Fanning and her readers' advice on sewing machines.*

Fiberarts, 50 College Street, Asheville, North Carolina 28801-2896, *artist fiber works, exhibitions, and ads for supplies.*

The Quilter's Newsletter.

Sew News, P.O. Box 1790, Peoria, Illinois 61656, *tailoring, fitting and sewing techniques, and many ads for supplies and services.*

Threads Magazine, Taunton Press, 63 South Main Street, P.O. Box 5506, Newtown, Connecticut 06470-5506, *articles on all fiber arts, ads for products, supplies, services and exhibitions.*

INDEX